MORE ADVANCE PRAISE FOR THE THIRD EDITION OF FOSTERING SUSTAINA[...]

" Fostering Sustainable Behavior *is a must-read for anyone interesting in impro[...] community-based behavior change programs. Students and professionals alike fin[...] practical, evidence-based advice both easy to grasp and easy to implement.*

Edward Maibach, MPH, Ph.D., Director
CENTER FOR CLIMATE CHANGE COMMUNICATION
GEORGE MASON UNIVERSITY

" *At Bicycle Victoria we're passionate about bike riding. We used to unleash that passion on others through convincing verbal arguments about why they should ride. We'd then shake our heads in disbelief when they didn't get on their bike. Then we discovered* Fostering Sustainable Behavior. *It has given us an effective and measurable way to get more people riding. Thanks to CBSM we're now closer to making bike riding normal. The great news is people are getting on their bikes without us having to convince them!*

Craig Richards, Chief Operating Officer
BICYCLE VICTORIA, MELBOURNE, AUSTRALIA

" *Encouraging behavior change on any scale is challenging and requires the application of well-proven models and theory. Community-based social marketing, developed by Doug McKenzie-Mohr, is a model that we have used successfully for nearly a decade in our programs. CBSM allows us to develop a comprehensive understanding of our target's barriers to change and what motivators are required to encourage the adoption of sustainable behaviors. Importantly the CBSM research process allows us to clearly demonstrate to decision makers that solid social science underpins our work and that excellent outcomes can and will be achieved.*

Greg Allen, Manager Community Education
DEPARTMENT OF ENVIRONMENT AND CONSERVATION
PERTH, WESTERN AUSTRALIA

" *I can't think of a more useful resource for anyone interested in helping communities adopt more sustainable behaviors. My students love the concise, research-based content, the clear how-to steps for designing and evaluating programs, and the many examples. I love that the author has continued to improve this classic text with more about how to select the target behaviors and how to encourage social diffusion. This book is a true gem and the new version is the best yet.*

Carol D. Saunders, Ph.D.
DEPT. OF ENVIRONMENTAL STUDIES
ANTIOCH UNIVERSITY NEW ENGLAND

Fostering Sustainable Behavior guided the development of our programs to tackle climate change in Wales. Doug's writing and thinking helped us to clarify not only which behaviors to target, but also how to create effective programs to foster emission reduction behaviors. We recommend this excellent book to agencies who are developing similar programs.

Usha Ladwa-Thomas
CLIMATE CHANGE AND WATER DIVISION
WELSH ASSEMBLY GOVERNMENT

Doug's book *Fostering Sustainable Behavior* was the single, most significant influence in the design of our residential water and energy efficiency programs. The Home WaterWise and ClimateSmart Home services each reached over 200,000 households in Queensland. The book not only expertly guides you through his research, but it outlines strategies and methods to achieve long-term behavior change, underpinned by real examples. It provides a compelling case to embrace a community-based social marketing approach as the key driver to engagement and ultimately, advocacy. We followed the principles outlined in the book and not only do the savings speak for themselves, but the engagement, advocacy and rates of participation are all testament to the success of this approach.

Anthony Coates, Exec. Director Major Projects
LOCAL GOVERNMENT INFRASTRUCTURE SERVICES
BRISBANE, QUEENSLAND

Doug's first edition of *Fostering Sustainable Behavior* put community-based social marketing on the map. His second edition launched it as a practical and powerful tool to influence behaviors to protect the environment. This third edition will ensure the principles and practices permanently orbit the globe.

Nancy R. Lee, President
SOCIAL MARKETING SERVICES, INC.

Fostering Sustainable Behavior is a must-read for anyone involved in energy and environmental policies and programs. McKenzie-Mohr's approach is solidly based in research and in many years of on-the-ground successful programs with careful evaluations. His discussion about the critical importance of carefully selecting and defining the behaviors and deeply understanding the barriers/benefits before moving to program or policy design - expanded in this edition - is essential. I highly recommend Fostering Sustainable Behavior and his highly informative website on community-based social marketing.

Linda Schuck, Founder and Chair
BEHAVIOR, ENERGY & CLIMATE CHANGE CONFERENCE

FOSTERING SUSTAINABLE BEHAVIOR

An Introduction to Community-Based Social Marketing

Doug McKenzie-Mohr, Ph.D.

NEW SOCIETY PUBLISHERS

Cover design by Steve Norell, Creative Soapbox.
Water droplet image © Shutterstock Images, Ben Heys,
Earth reflection, NASA, Wikimedia Commons.

Printed in Canada. First printing February 2011.

New Society Publishers acknowledges the support of the
Government of Canada through the Book Publishing Industry
Development Program (BPIDP) for our publishing activities.

Paperback ISBN: 978-0-86571-642-1
eISBN: 978-1-55092-462-6

Inquiries regarding requests to reprint all or part of *Fostering Sustainable Behavior*
should be addressed to New Society Publishers at the address below. To order directly
from the publishers, please call toll-free (North America) 1-800-567-6772,
or order online at www.newsociety.com

Any other inquiries can be directed by mail to:
New Society Publishers P.O. Box 189, Gabriola Island, BC V0R 1X0, Canada
(250) 247-9737

New Society Publishers' mission is to publish books that contribute in fundamental
ways to building an ecologically sustainable and just society, and to do so with the
least possible impact on the environment, in a manner that models this vision. We are
committed to doing this not just through education, but through action. Our printed,
bound books are printed on Forest Stewardship Council-certified acid-free paper that
is 100% post-consumer recycled (100% old growth forest-free), processed chlorine free,
and printed with vegetable-based, low-VOC inks, with covers produced using FSC-
certified stock. New Society also works to reduce its carbon footprint, and purchases
carbon offsets based on an annual audit to ensure a carbon neutral footprint. For further information, or to browse our full list of books and purchase securely, visit our
website at: www.newsociety.com

Library and Archives Canada Cataloguing in Publication

McKenzie-Mohr, Doug, 1959-
         Fostering sustainable behavior : an introduction to community- based
social marketing / Doug McKenzie-Mohr. – 3rd ed.

ISBN 978-0-86571-642-1

         1. Social marketing. 2. Sustainable development. 3. Behavior
modification. I. Title.

HF5415.M35 2011   303.48'4   C2011-900490-9

NEW SOCIETY PUBLISHERS
www.newsociety.com

For my daughters, Jaime and Taryn, and my partner, Sue.
Three constant sources of support, joy and love in my life.

Contents

Preface

L es Milbrath was fond of reminding me that "nature bats last." What Les meant by this was that we live in a finite world and humanity will eventually be forced to adopt sustainable practices. While we have no choice regarding whether we eventually adopt these practices, the speed with which they are adopted will determine the grace with which we make this transition.

This book is about making the transition gracefully. It provides a comprehensive introduction to community-based social marketing and how it is being applied throughout the world to foster sustainable behavior. It introduces the five steps of community-based social marketing (selecting behaviors, identifying barriers & benefits, developing strategies, conducting a pilot, and broad-scale implementation), and showcases numerous programs illustrating its use. In this third edition, each chapter has been updated. Further, *Selecting Behaviors* has been added as a new first step in community-based social marketing. As well, a new behavior change tool—social diffusion—has been added to the array of tools already covered.

Community-based social marketing draws heavily on research in social psychology, which indicates that initiatives to promote behavior change are often most effective when they are carried out at the community level and involve direct contact with people. The emergence of community-based social marketing can be traced to a growing understanding that programs that rely heavily or exclusively on media advertising can be effective in creating public awareness and understanding of issues related to sustainability, but are limited in their ability to foster behavior change.

For those who are contemplating entering this field, I would like to offer the following words of encouragement. I have been fortunate over the past twenty-five years to work at the juncture between social science knowledge and its application to sustainability. I've had the opportunity to travel extensively discussing community-based social marketing with those who develop programs and with academics that work to advance our knowledge in this area. I have witnessed repeatedly the commitment and passion that both practitioners and academics bring to working on these issues. As daunting as our present circumstances may seem, know that there are countless individuals working on fostering sustainable behavior and that their efforts are making a difference. There are substantive and meaningful contributions to be made to the transition to sustainability. Come join us in helping humanity make this transition more gracefully.

Doug McKenzie-Mohr, Ph.D.
December 2010

How to Use this Book

Throughout this book you will find icons whose purpose is to draw your attention to specific information. Below is a guide to their meaning.

 Take home messages. If you forget everything else in this book, remember these.

 Something worth noting. Less important than the take home messages, but still important.

 Information related to utilzing the community-based social marketing website (http://www.cbsm.com).

 Information related to the discussion forums at cbsm.com.

 Information related to the areas of agriculture and conservation.

 Information related to energy.

 Information related to transportation.

 Information related to waste reduction and pollution.

 Information related to water efficiency or watershed protection.

Fostering
Sustainable Behavior

> " *That which is not good for the beehive*
> *cannot be good for the bees.*
>
> **Marcus Aurelius**

When my wife and I moved to Fredericton, Canada we bought a composter for our backyard. During the first summer and fall in our new home we fed the composter diligently. However, by January a snow drift three feet deep stretched from our back door to the composter. I started off the month with good intentions, shoveling a pathway or trampling down the snow with a pair of winter boots that reached nearly to my knees, but by late January, when the temperature dropped to minus 30°F, I had had enough, and despite my good intentions, the organics ended up in the garbage can at the curbside.

My environmental transgressions extend beyond seasonal composting. While I was still teaching, I would bike to work during the spring, summer and fall. However, during the winter, which in Fredericton stretches from November through to early April, I would take a taxi. I knew that automobiles are a principal source of the carbon dioxide emissions that lead to global warming, so why didn't

I walk to work or take the bus? To walk to work took approximately 30 minutes. While the exercise would have been good for me, I would rather have spent that time with my family. As for the bus, there was no direct bus route from our house to the university—making it slower to take the bus than to walk. Finally, the taxi cost only marginally more than bus fare, making it an even easier choice to take the taxi. While concerned about climate change, my behavior for six months of the year was inconsistent with my concern.

These two anecdotes illustrate the challenges faced in making our communities more sustainable. Composting can significantly reduce the municipal solid waste stream, but only if people elect to compost. Mass transit can reduce carbon dioxide emissions, and urban air pollution, but only if people leave their cars at home and take the bus or train instead. People play an equally critical role in many other sustainable activities. Programmable thermostats can reduce home heating costs and also carbon dioxide emissions, but only if people install and program them. Water efficient toilets and shower heads can significantly reduce residential water use, but only if people have them installed. The purchase of environmentally friendly products can significantly affect our environment, but once again, only if people elect to alter their purchase habits.

How important are changes in individual behavior? Thomas Dietz and his colleagues have estimated that it is possible to reduce total U.S. CO_2 emissions by 7.4% over the next ten years through programs that target residential energy use and nonbusiness travel.[2] Not only is this a significant reduction in emissions, but they also note that it can be obtained much more quickly than reductions in emissions through other means, such as building more fuel-efficient vehicles or transitioning to renewable energy, as these changes will take time to accomplish. This *behavioral wedge*, they argue, buys us time as we put in place policies that will significantly reduce future emissions.

Behavioral choices play an equally critical role in the commercial and agricultural sectors. In the commercial sector, day-to-day behaviors have a substantial impact upon emissions, energy and water use, and waste produced. Similarly, daily choices in the agricultural sector have significant impacts in a variety of areas, including CO_2 emissions and agricultural runoff.

BEHAVIOR MATTERS

Behavior change is the corner-stone of sustainability. Whether you are working on protecting wetlands, enhancing water or energy efficiency, altering modal transportation choices, or any of the myriad of other behaviors related to sustainability, behavior change matters. Changes in behavior not only directly affect our progress toward sustainability, but they can also power-fully affect how people view themselves.[1] For example, when people engage in actions that reduce CO_2 emissions, such as turning off their vehicle engines, they are likely to come to see themselves as the type of person who cares about climate change based upon their engagement in the behavior. These changes in how they view themselves can significantly affect their support for policy changes.

INFORMATION-BASED CAMPAIGNS

Most programs to foster sustainable behavior rely upon large-scale information campaigns. These campaigns are usually based on one of two perspectives regarding changing behavior. The first perspective, which is referred to as the *Attitude-Behavior* approach, assumes that changes in behavior are brought about by increasing public knowledge about an issue, such as climate change, and by fostering attitudes that are supportive of a desired activity, such as taking the bus rather than driving. Accordingly, programs based on this perspective attempt to alter behavior by providing information, through media advertising, and frequently the distribution of brochures, flyers and newsletters. The second perspective, which we will come to later, is referred to as the *Economic Self-Interest* approach.

ATTITUDE-BEHAVIOR APPROACH

Is it warranted to believe that by enhancing knowledge, or altering attitudes, behavior will change? Apparently not. Numerous studies document that education alone often has little or no effect upon sustainable behavior. The following are examples:

▶ Scott Geller and his colleagues studied the impact that intensive workshops have upon residential energy conservation.[3] In these workshops, participants were exposed to three hours of educational material in a variety of formats (slide shows, lectures, etc.). All of the material had been designed to impress upon participants that it was possible to reduce home energy use significantly. Geller measured the impact of the workshops by testing participants' attitudes and beliefs prior to, and following, the workshops. Upon completing the workshop, attendees indicated greater awareness of energy issues, more appreciation for what could be done in their homes to reduce energy use, and a willingness to implement the changes that were advocated in the workshop. Despite these changes in awareness and attitudes, behavior did not change. In follow-up visits to the homes of the 40 workshop participants, only one had followed through on the recommendation to lower the hot water thermostat. Two participants had put insulating blankets around their hot water heaters, but they had done so prior to attending the workshop.

BEYOND BROCHURES

Numerous studies document that education alone often has little or no effect upon sustainable behavior. As a consequence, programs that make use of information intensive approaches, such as bill-stuffers, flyers, and direct mail have very little likelihood of changing behavior.

In fact, the only difference between the 40 workshop participants and an equal number of non-participants was in the installation of water-efficient shower heads. Eight of the 40 participants had installed them, while two of the non-participants had. However, the installation of the water-efficient shower heads was not due to education alone. Each of the workshop participants had been given a *free* water-efficient shower head to install.

► A study conducted in the Netherlands revealed that providing households with information about energy conservation did not reduce energy use.[4]

► High school students who received a six-day workshop that focused on creating awareness of environmental issues were found, in a two-month follow-up, to be no more likely to have engaged in pro-environmental actions.[5]

► Households who volunteered to participate in a ten-week study of water-use received a state-of-the-art handbook on water efficiency. The handbook described wasteful water-use, explained the relationship between water-use and energy consumption, and detailed methods for conserving water in the home. Despite great attention being paid to the preparation of the handbook, it was found to have no impact upon consumption.[6]

► Canada's national effort to reduce CO_2 emissions in the residential sector, the One-Tonne Challenge, relied heavily on media advertising. An audit of its effectiveness indicated that 51% of Canadians knew of the program, but few changed their behavior.[7]

The above studies document that information campaigns that emphasize enhancing knowledge or altering attitudes frequently have little or no effect upon behavior. The following studies provide further evidence of the ineffectiveness of this approach. If increasing knowledge and altering attitudes result in behavior change, we should expect measures of attitudes and knowledge to be closely associated with behavior. As shown below, however, there is often little or no relationship between attitudes and/or knowledge, and behavior.

▶ A survey of participants in a voluntary auto-emissions inspection program revealed that they did not differ in their attitudes toward, or knowledge regarding, air pollution compared to a random sample of individuals who had not had their car inspected.[8]

▶ When some 500 people were interviewed and asked about personal responsibility for picking up litter, 94% acknowledged that individuals bore a responsibility for picking up litter. However, when leaving the interview, only 2% picked up litter that had been *planted* by the researcher.[9]

▶ Two large surveys of Swiss respondents found that environmental information, knowledge and awareness were poorly associated with environmental behavior.[10]

▶ In one study, individuals who held attitudes that were strongly supportive of energy conservation were found to be no more likely to conserve energy.[11]

▶ An investigation of differences between recyclers and non-recyclers found that they did not differ in their attitudes toward recycling.[12]

While environmental attitudes and knowledge have been found to be related to behavior, as the above examples demonstrate the relationship is frequently weak or nonexistent. Why would attitudes and knowledge not be more strongly related to behavior? Consider the two anecdotes with which I began this chapter. I have attitudes that are supportive of both composting and alternative transportation. Further, I am relatively knowledgeable on both of these topics. Nevertheless, in both cases another factor—inconvenience brought on by winter—moderated whether my attitudes and knowledge were predictive of my behavior. In short, a variety of barriers can deter individuals from engaging in a sustainable behavior. Lack of knowledge and unsupportive attitudes are only two of these barriers.

INFORMATION'S ROLE

Programs that are strictly information-based have little likelihood of substantively changing behavior. Nonetheless, this does not mean that providing information should not be a component of a behavior change program, only that by itself information is unlikely to be effective. The critical question to ask is, "How does providing information address barriers to a target audience engaging in the behavior I wish to encourage?"

ECONOMIC SELF-INTEREST APPROACH

The second perspective assumes that individuals systematically evaluate choices, such as whether to install additional insulation to an attic or purchase a high efficiency showerhead, and then act in accordance with their economic self-interest. This perspective suggests that in order to affect these decisions, an organization, such as a utility, need only provide information to the public that something is in their financial best interest and consequently the public will behave accordingly. However, as with information campaigns that focus on altering knowledge and attitudes, efforts that have concentrated on underscoring the financial advantages of a sustainable activity, such as installing a low-flow shower head or adding insulation, have also been largely unsuccessful. Here are two examples:

▶ Annually, California utilities spend 200 million dollars on advertising to encourage energy conservation. These advertisements encourage householders to install energy-conserving devices and adopt habits, such as closing the blinds during the day, that will decrease energy use. Despite massive expenditures, these campaigns have had little effect on energy use.[13]

▶ An act passed by the United States Congress brought into being the Residential Conservation Service (RCS). The RCS mandated that major gas and electric utilities in the United States provide homeowners with audits in order to enhance energy efficiency. In addition, homeowners had access to interest-free or low-cost loans and a listing of local contractors and suppliers. In total, 5.6% of eligible households requested that an RCS assessor evaluate their home.[14] Of those who had their home evaluated, 50% took steps to enhance the energy efficiency of their dwelling, compared to 30% for non-participants (the non-participants were households who were on the waiting list to have their homes assessed).[15] What types of actions were taken? In general, the actions were inexpensive and did not involve a contractor. Frequent energy-efficiency actions included caulking, weather-stripping, installing programmable thermostats, turning down the hot water thermostat, and installing a water heater blanket. These actions reduced energy use per

BEYOND ECONOMICS

Economic incentives can increase motivation for someone to adopt a sustainable behavior, but it does not address the barriers to the behavior being adopted. For example, a rebate on purchasing a programmable thermostat might increase the number of people who purchase these thermostats, but it does nothing to address the barriers to installing the thermostat or programming it.

household between 2% and 3%.[16] Given that millions of dollars were spent on the RCS, and that it is possible to reduce residential energy use often by more than 20%, an initiative that produces annual savings of 2-3% can only be seen as a failure.

Why did such a comprehensive program fail? In large part the RCS failed because it did not pay adequate attention to the *human* side of promoting more sustainable energy use. Those who designed this massive initiative assumed that homeowners would retrofit their homes if it was clear that it was in their financial best interest to do so. While this economic perspective does consider the human side of sustainable behavior, it does so in a very simplistic way. As a United States National Research Council study concluded, this view of human behavior overlooks "…the rich mixture of cultural practices, social interactions, and human feelings that influence the behavior of individuals, social groups, and institutions."[17]

THE EFFECT OF INFORMATION CAMPAIGNS

Information campaigns proliferate because it is relatively easy to distribute printed materials or air radio or television advertising.[18] Advertising, however, is often an extremely expensive way of reaching people. In one distressing case, a California utility spent more money on advertising the benefits of installing insulation in low-income housing than it would have cost to upgrade the insulation in the targeted houses.[19] As Mark Costanzo points out, "Although advertising is an important tool for creating awareness, it is wasteful to invest most of our efforts in an influence strategy that has such a low probability of success."[20] The failure of mass media campaigns to foster sustainable behavior is due in part to the poor design of the messages, but more importantly to an underestimation of the difficulty of changing behavior.[21] Costanzo and his colleagues note that most mass media efforts to promote sustainable behavior are based on traditional marketing techniques in which the sustainable activity is viewed as a "product" to be sold. Advertising, they note, is effective in altering our preference to purchase one brand over another. However, altering consumer preferences is not creating new behavior, rather it involves altering an existing behavior. As they indicate, "These small changes in behavior generally require little expense or effort and no dramatic change in lifestyle" (p. 526). In contrast, encouraging individuals to engage in a new activity, such as walking or biking to work, is much more complex. A variety of barriers to walking or biking to work exist, such as concerns over time, safety, weather, and convenience. The diversity of barriers which exist for any sustainable activity means that information campaigns alone will rarely bring about behavior change.

To date, too little attention has been paid to ensuring that the programs we implement have a high likelihood of actually changing behavior. The cornerstone of sustainability is delivering programs that are effective in changing people's behavior. If we are to make the transition to a sustainable future gracefully, we must concern ourselves with what leads individuals to engage in behavior that collectively is sustainable, and design our programs accordingly.

AN ALTERNATIVE: COMMUNITY-BASED SOCIAL MARKETING
Community-based social marketing is an attractive alternative to information-intensive campaigns. In contrast to conventional approaches, community-based social marketing has been shown to be very effective at bringing about behavior change. Its effectiveness is due to its pragmatic approach. This approach involves: carefully selecting the behavior to be promoted; identifying the barriers and benefits associated with the selected behavior; designing a strategy that utilizes behavior-change tools to address these barriers and benefits; piloting the strategy with a small segment of a community; and, finally; evaluating the impact of the program once it has been implemented broadly.

▶ **STEP 1: SELECTING BEHAVIORS:** Whether the purpose of campaign is to reduce waste, enhance energy or water efficiency, alter transportation choices, protect a watershed or reduce CO_2 emissions, there are nearly always a wide array of behaviors that may be promoted. For example, if the purpose was to reduce residential energy use, this goal might be achieved by encouraging the installation of insulation in an attic, installing and setting a programmable thermostat or taking shorter showers. Similarly, there are numerous behaviors that could be encouraged related to water use, transportation, waste reduction, etc. The first step of community-based social marketing is to determine which of these behaviors should be promoted.

▶ **STEP 2: IDENTIFYING BARRIERS AND BENEFITS:** If any form of sustainable behavior is to be widely adopted, barriers that impede people from engaging in the activity must first be identified along with what would motivate them to act. Community-based social marketers begin by identifying these barriers and benefits using a combination of literature reviews, observations, focus groups, and survey research. The barriers they identify may be internal to the individual, such as lack of knowledge regarding how to carry out an activity (e.g., composting), or external, as in structural changes that need to be made in order for the behavior to be more convenient (e.g., organizing carpooling amongst employees).[22] Community-based social marketers recognize that there may be multiple internal and external barriers to widespread participation in any form of sustainable behavior and that these barriers will vary for different individuals. For example, personal safety is more likely to be a concern to women as they consider using mass transit than it is for men. In contrast to the *Attitude-Behavior* and *Economic Self-Interest* perspectives just discussed, community-based social marketers attempt to remove as many of these barriers as possible. Social science research indicates that the barriers that prevent individuals from engaging in one form of sustainable behavior, such as adding insulation to an attic, often have little in common with the barriers that keep individuals from engaging in other forms of sustainable behavior, such as carpooling.[23] Further, this research demonstrates that even within a class of sustainable activities, such as waste reduction, very different barriers emerge as being important.[24] For example, different barriers exist for recycling, composting, or source reduction. Since the barriers that prevent individuals from engaging in sustainable behavior are activity-specific, community-based social marketers begin to develop a strategy only after they have identified a particular activity's barriers and benefits. Once these barriers and benefits have been identified, they develop a social marketing strategy to remove the barriers and enhance the benefits.

BUILDING SUPPORT

Barriers exist not just to behaviors we wish to promote, but also to the very use of community-based social marketing. This approach is often a dramatic departure for organizations that are used to delivering information-intensive campaigns. Building support within an agency for utilizing community-based social marketing is discussed in the last chapter of this book.

▶ **STEP 3: DEVELOPING STRATEGIES:** Social science research has identified a variety of "tools" that are effective in changing behavior. These tools include approaches such as gaining a commitment from an individual that they will try a new activity, such as biking to work, or developing community norms that encourage people to behave more sustainably. The techniques that are used by community-based social marketers are carried out at the community level and frequently involve direct personal contact. Personal contact is emphasized because social science research indicates that we are most likely to change our behavior in response to direct appeals from others.

▶ **STEP 4: PILOTING:** Prior to implementing a community-based social marketing strategy, it is piloted in a small portion of a community. Given the high cost of implementing many programs, it is essential to know that a strategy will work before it is implemented on a large scale. Conducting a pilot allows a program to be refined until it is effective. Further, a pilot allows other possible methods for carrying out a project to be tested against one another and the most cost-effective method to be determined. Finally, conducting a pilot can be a crucial step in demonstrating to funders the worthiness of implementing a program on a broad scale.

▶ **STEP 5: BROAD-SCALE IMPLEMENTATION AND EVALUATION:** The final step of community-based social marketing involves ongoing evaluation of a program once it has been implemented in a community. In conducting an evaluation, community-based social marketers emphasize the direct measurement of behavior-change over less direct measures such as self-reports or increases in awareness. The information gleaned from evaluation can be used to refine the marketing strategy further as well as provide evidence that a project should receive further funding.

The following chapters detail the five steps of community-based social marketing. After reading these chapters, you will have the information you need to create programs that can have a substantial impact on the adoption of sustainable behaviors in your community.

PILOTING

Frequently programs are not pilot-tested prior to be implementing broadly. Without conducting a pilot we cannot be confident that the program will change behavior or do so cost-effectively.

Step 1: Selecting Behaviors

> *" Advice is what we ask for when we already know the answer but wish we didn't.*
>
> **Erica Jong**

Whether you are developing a program to promote water efficiency, waste reduction, watershed protection, energy efficiency, modal transportation shifts, or virtually any other area related to sustainability, you will encounter the same problem—there is a multitude of behaviors that may be targeted. In the case of energy efficiency, we might encourage home owners to add additional insulation to their attics or wash their clothes in cold water. We might encourage employees of local businesses to turn off their computers when not in use, or have farmers sell their produce at local markets. These are just a few of the many energy-efficient actions that might be promoted. Since it is common to have a variety of behaviors that we might foster, it is important to be able to make informed choices regarding which are the most worthwhile to target.

Imagine that you are assigned the task of designing a program to encourage energy efficiency. More specifically, your program is being funded to reduce CO_2 emissions through more efficient energy use.

START WITH SECTORS

The selection of behaviors begins by determining which sectors have the greatest impact on your area of interest. Once you have determined which sector(s) to target, analyze how your issue is affected by the different behaviors within that sector.

The first question that you will want to ask is, "Which sector makes the most sense to target?" In Canada, non-transportation related energy use is a follows: industrial (55%), residential (23%), commercial/ institutional (18%) and agriculture (3%).[1] If you were delivering your program in Canada you would understandably gravitate toward those Canadian sectors that have the largest energy use. In considering these sectors you might elect to focus on residential energy use as this sector uses a significant amount of energy. In addition, you know of a number of organizations that you can partner with to target this sector more effectively. Having decided upon the sector, your next task is to evaluate which behaviors within this sector are worth promoting.

To determine which behaviors to promote, begin by creating a list of residential energy efficiency behaviors. Note, however, that an Australian project found that there were over 200 behaviors related to residential energy efficiency.[2] While the number of residential energy efficiency behaviors is vast, don't be surprised if lists for other domains (e.g., water efficiency, transportation, conservation) are also sizable. Since we are understandably interested in those behaviors that can have a substantive impact upon energy use, it makes sense first to determine if some areas of residential energy use are more important than others. If this is case, we may be able shorten our list by focusing our attention on those areas that account for the most significant energy use.

As the following chart demonstrates, Canadian residential energy use differs markedly by end use.[3] Given its northern climate, the largest share of residential energy use is for space heating (63%), followed by water heating (18%) and then major appliances (13%). Collectively, these three categories account for 94% of Canadian residential energy use. Interestingly, the two categories that traditionally receive significant attention in Canadian energy efficiency programs, lighting and air conditioning, use relatively little energy—4% and 2%, respectively. Knowing that space heating, water heating and major appliances dominate Canadian residential energy use suggests the order your most impactful behaviors are likely to follow. Without additional research you won't know *which* behaviors within these categories are most impactful, for example adding additional insulation to the walls of a home versus installing energy efficient windows, but you will have greater confidence that your behaviors are drawn from the most important categories.

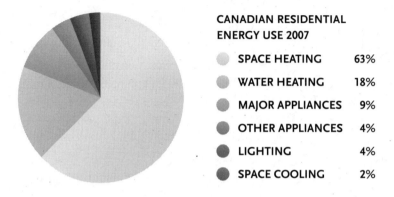

CANADIAN RESIDENTIAL ENERGY USE 2007

SPACE HEATING	63%
WATER HEATING	18%
MAJOR APPLIANCES	9%
OTHER APPLIANCES	4%
LIGHTING	4%
SPACE COOLING	2%

Once you have determined which categories of energy use are most important, you are ready to begin creating your list of behaviors. Each behavior that you list should be guided by two criteria: no behavior should be *divisible*; and each behavior should be *end-state*. Both are described below.

DIVISIBLE BEHAVIORS: Divisible behaviors refer to those actions that can be divided further. For instance, many residential energy efficiency programs encourage adding additional insulation as a way to reduce home energy use substantially. However, adding additional insulation to a home can be further divided into adding insulation to the attic, the external shell (walls), or the basement. Why does it matter that a list of residential energy-efficiency behaviors specify adding insulation to attics, walls and basements rather than just adding additional insulation? Each of these behaviors differ substantively in the barriers that are associated with them. I recently added insulation to our attic to improve the energy efficiency of our home and reduce its CO_2 footprint. This was a fairly simple process that involved a contractor blowing additional insulation into our attic. Completing the task took the contractor several hours and was relatively inexpensive. In contrast, adding additional insulation to the external shell of our home involved substantial cost, time

BARRIERS MATTER

Because barriers are often behavior-specific, it is critical to begin with a list of non-divisible behaviors. Failure to ensure that behaviors are non-divisible will make developing effective behavior-change strategies far more difficult.

and effort. First, our existing siding had to be removed. Our house was then wrapped to reduce heat loss, additional insulation was added over the house wrap and, finally, our home was re-sided. The renovations to the external shell of our home took over a month. While the renovations to our attic and the shell of our home both involved adding insulation, they differed dramatically in their associated barriers. Since the barriers to sustainable behaviors are *often* behavior-specific, it is critical to begin by listing behaviors that are non-divisible. Failing to do so will leave you with categories of behaviors in which the behaviors that make up a category (e.g., adding insulation to a home) may differ dramatically in their associated barriers and benefits.

The divisibility of behaviors needs to be carefully considered. Adding additional insulation to an attic, for example, is also divisible. We need to specify whether it will be a contractor or home owner who will install the additional insulation, as well as the type of insulation to be installed. Why does this matter? In Canada, there are two primary forms of insulation that homeowners add to their attics: fiberglass batts and cellulose fibre. In the case of fiberglass batts, either a home owner or a contractor would purchase the batts from a hardware store and then add the additional insulation to the attic. However, blowing cellulose fibre into an attic is significantly more challenging for a home owner than it is for a contractor.

Contractors who blow insulation into attics tend to have vans that are outfitted for this purpose. In the back of their van they will have a motor for blowing the insulation as well as several hundred feet of hose that can reach from a driveway to an attic. For a home owner to blow insulation into their attic they would need to rent the blower and hose and have a vehicle that was large enough to carry these, and the insulation, back to their home. In addition, they need to know how to use the rented equipment. Clearly, the barriers to a home owner blowing insulation into their attic are substantially higher than for having a contractor do the same work. As a consequence, a list of residential energy-efficient behaviors would distinguish between whether a contractor or home owner was blowing insulation into an attic. Similarly, this list would also distinguish between contractor or a home owner was adding fiberglass batts to an attic. At this point you might be thinking that community-based social marketing is rigid in its approach to selecting behaviors. It is, but for good reason. Failure to create a list of non-divisible behaviors will jeopardize the development of effective strategies as there will be insufficient information regarding the barriers to specific behaviors.

END-STATE BEHAVIORS: In addition to your behaviors being non-divisible, you also need verify that they are end-state. End-state refers to the behavior that actually produces the desired environmental outcome. For instance, the purchase of compact fluorescent light bulbs or the installation of programmable thermostats are not end-state behaviors. Our principal interest is not in having homeowners *purchase* compact fluorescent light bulbs, but rather in having them *install* them.[†] Similarly, our principal interest is not in having homeowners *install* programmable thermostats, but rather in having them *program* them. Frequently, environmental programs encourage *prior* behaviors and fail to achieve the *end-state* behavioral changes that matter. To determine whether a behavior is end-state, simply ask:"Will engaging in this behavior produce the desired environmental outcome, or will the target audience need to do something else before the desired outcome is achieved?" If they need to engage in another behavior before the desired environmental outcome is achieved, you have *not* selected an end-state behavior.

Having created a list of non-divisible, end-state residential energy efficiency behaviors drawn primarily from the categories of space heating, water heating and major appliances, your next task is to compare these behaviors to determine which are worth promoting. This involves analyzing the following three characteristics of each behavior: 1) How *impactful* is the behavior? 2) How *probable* is it that my target audience will engage in the behavior? and 3) What level of *penetration* has the behavior already obtained with my target audience?

NO STRATEGIES

When creating a list of end-state, non-divisible behaviors ensure that no item on the list is a strategy (e.g., encouraging home owners to engage in an energy audit). Listing strategies assumes that you already know enough about the barriers and benefits that are associated with the behaviors you wish to promote to determine effective strategies. Unless you have carried out the barrier and benefit research covered in the next chapter, this is a questionable assumption.

---

† In a project that I served as an advisor on in Queensland, Australia homeowners were given a number of compact fluorescent light bulbs (CFLs), but only if they first gave the electrician who visited their home an equal number of incandescent light bulbs. This exchange of light bulbs was incorporated into the program to ensure that the end-state behavior of having the homeowner install the CFLs was achieved.

MULTIPLE IMPACTS

If you are interested in more than one impact, such as reducing CO_2 emissions and promoting cardiovascular health, collect information on both impacts for your list of behaviors. You can then use this information to select those behaviors that have substantive impacts for both areas.

CASES & REPORTS

Search the Fostering Sustainable Behavior website's (cbsm.com) cases and reports databases for reviews of programs that fostered specific behavioral changes.

DETERMINING IMPACT

Two methods exist for determining the impact of the listed behaviors. The first, and preferred method, involves collecting information. Remembering that in our hypothetical example, your program is being funded to reduce CO_2 emissions, you would need to assess the emission reductions that are associated with each of the residential behaviors you have listed. For example, you would collect information on the emissions associated with such diverse behaviors as installing and configuring a programmable thermostat, turning down the water heater temperature, washing clothes in cold water, etc. When reliable information regarding the impact of these behaviors does not exist, you can estimate the impacts using the second method.

To estimate the impact of any particular behavior, you should survey individuals who have expertise regarding residential energy use and ask them to rate each behavior on a five-point scale of 0 to 4, where "0" equals "no impact" and "4" equals "significant impact." Note that your ratings will be more reliable if your experts rate the behaviors independently and you average the results afterwards. You should avoid amassing a group of experts to discuss the behaviors before they rate them. Group ratings are more likely to be biased than ratings that are done individually and then averaged. When individuals rate the impact of a behavior, some will overestimate its impact while others will underestimate it. These errors tend be distributed like a normal curve and, consequently, cancel each other out when averaged. Averaged individual ratings often have superior psychometric properties to group ratings.

DETERMINING PROBABILITY

Two methods also exist for determining probability. The preferred method is to examine past programs to assess how effective they were in encouraging specific behavioral changes. In reviewing these programs, collect information not only regarding what percentage adopted the behavioral change, but also how the program was delivered, the context within which the program was delivered (e.g., does a community have high energy costs which would provide additional motivation for them to adopt energy efficiency behaviors?), and the cost to deliver the program. For each behavior you are likely to find a variety of programs which vary in each of these areas as well as with respect to the percentage who adopted the behavioral change. This information can provide clues regarding what level of adoption may be associated with different types of programs, as well as provide insight into the costs associated with achieving different levels of adoption.

While investigating past programs provides the most reliable information regarding probabilities, what if your list of behaviors is very long? In this case the second method should be used. The second method for determining probability involves surveying your target audience and asking them to rate the probability that they would engage in a variety of behaviors. To obtain these ratings, use a scale of 0 to 4, where "0" equals "no likelihood" and "4" equals "high likelihood." For these ratings to be meaningful, you will need to provide some context for the questions. For example, rather than simply asking, "How likely are you to install a high-efficiency shower head?" you should ask several questions that set out different contexts (e.g., How likely are you to install a high-efficiency shower head if you had to purchase and install it yourself? How likely are you to install a high-efficiency shower head if you were supplied with a shower head, but had to install it yourself? and How likely would you be to install a high-efficiency shower head if you were supplied with a shower head and it was installed for you?).

You should survey a representative sample of your target audience to ensure that the obtained probabilities are indicative of your community. However, even if your survey is representative of your community, you still need to be careful in interpreting survey data. It is likely that survey participants will *inflate* their stated likelihood of engaging in the behaviors in your survey. As a consequence, you should compare the relative probabilities in your survey rather than the absolute numbers. If 50% of your participants say that they would install weather-stripping that number is likely inflated. However, if in contrast, 20% of your participants indicate that they would purchase an energy-efficient fridge, we can be relatively confident that weather-stripping is more probable than fridge purchases, even if we can't be confident of what the exact probabilities are.

Finally, it should be noted that you can combine both the research

GETTING HELP

The discussion forums on the Fostering Sustainable Behavior website (cbsm.com) are a wonderful resource for tracking down information on how effectively specific behavioral changes have been fostered. Before posting a question to the forums, search past topics to see if the information you are looking for has already been discussed.

and survey methods. Rather than collecting program information on a large number of residential energy-efficient behaviors, you might begin by surveying your target audience to determine the probability of them engaging in each of these behaviors. This can be done quickly and relatively inexpensively. The probability information you obtain from the survey is then used to reduce your list to perhaps only those activities that have moderate to high probabilities associated with them. You then collect information on programs that have been delivered to foster the behaviors on this shorter list—a much more doable task than investigating a large number of behaviors.

DETERMINING PENETRATION

As with determining impact and probability, two methods also exist for determining penetration. If the behavior is observable, such as transit usage, curbside recycling, or bicycling, direct observations of the behavior can be used to determine the percentage of a target audience that have adopted the behavior. Unfortunately, many behaviors have little or no visibility. These include most behaviors related to residential energy-efficiency. In these cases, the second option is to survey the target audience to determine participation in the behavior. To save time and money, you can combine the surveys investigating probabilities and penetration.

If the behavior is a one-time action, such as installing insulation in an attic, simply ask if the behavior has been adopted. In contrast, if the behavior is repetitive, such as washing clothes in cold water, ask if the household engages in the action and, if so, how often. As with surveying target audiences regarding the probability of their engaging in a behavior, numbers obtained from these surveys are likely to be inflated.

COMBINING IMPACT, PROBABILITY AND PENETRATION

Having collected information regarding impacts, probabilities and penetration, you are now ready to select your behaviors. Select behaviors that have the best combination of impact, probability and penetration. More specifically, your program should focus on those behaviors that have high impact, high probability and low penetration. Why should you gravitate toward behaviors that have low penetration? If most people in your community have already adopted the behavior, you have little to gain by focusing on that action. Ideally, you will want to summarize the information in a table format, such as the one found below. Note that you can multiply the values that you have obtained for impact, probability and penetration, but that before you do you will need to invert the penetration values. For instance, if 20% of households have installed water efficient shower heads subtract this number from 1 to obtain the number that have yet to participate in the behavior (80%).

CALCULATING WEIGHTS[‡]

BEHAVIOR	IMPACT (KG/PER HOUSEHOLD/ YEAR)	PROBABILITY (0 TO 4)	PENETRATION (1 - VALUE)	WEIGHT
Purchase Green Power	8700	2.15	.85	15,899
Install 3 High Efficiency Shower heads	650	2.5	.35	569
Wash Clothes in Cold Water	450	3.09	.63	876

‡ On behalf of Local Government Infrastructure Services of Queensland, Australia, the Institute for Sustainable Futures estimated the CO_2 emission reductions associated with a variety of energy-efficiency behaviors. The probability values are from a state-wide survey conducted in Queensland, Australia by Local Government and Infrastructure Services. The penetration values are fabrications as these values were not available.

SUMMARY

As illustrated in this chapter, the selection of behaviors involves the following steps:

1. Collecting information regarding which sector(s) merit targeting;

2. Selecting a sector that makes a significant contribution to the issue you are trying to address;

3. Investigating which categories within that sector contribute most to your issue (e.g., Canadian residential space heating);

4. Creating a list of non-divisible, end-state behaviors that are drawn from the most important categories;

5. Determining the impact, probability and penetration levels for these non-divisible, end-state behaviors; and

6. Selecting those behaviors that have the best combination of impact, probability and penetration.

Too frequently, environmental programs are delivered simply because someone felt it would be worthwhile to promote a specific behavior. If we are to make greater progress in fostering sustainability, we need to be more rigorous in how we select behaviors. By focusing on those behaviors that have the best combination of impact, probability and penetration, we can be more assured that our programs will have the desired outcome.

Step 2: Identifying Barriers and Benefits

> *" Don't let us forget that the causes of human actions are usually immeasurably more complex than our subsequent explanations of them.*
>
> **Fyodor Dostoevsky**

We each have hunches about why people engage in activities such as walking to work, recycling or composting. For instance, theories regarding personal motivations for recycling abound. Recycling, it has been suggested, is popular because it serves to alleviate our guilt for not adopting the more difficult and inconvenient aspects of sustainable living. This hypothesis suggests that curbside recycling is simply an antidote to the guilt we feel when, for example, just after placing our recycling container at the curb, we hop into our own personal global warming factory and head off to work. Other theories suggest that individuals recycle because it is convenient, those around us recycle, it makes us feel good about ourselves, or we are simply badgered into it by our children.

Hunches regarding what motivates people to engage in sustainable behavior are important. However, these personal theories need to be identified for what they are: speculation. Speculation regarding what leads individuals to engage in responsible environmental behavior should never be used as the basis for a community-based social marketing plan. Prior to designing such a plan you need to set aside personal speculation and collect the information that will properly inform your efforts. To create an effective community-based social marketing strategy, you must be able to sort through the competing theories. In doing this, you will discover the actual barriers that inhibit individuals from engaging in the activity, as well as what would motivate them to act. Once you have this information, you are well-positioned to create an effective strategy. The purpose of this chapter, then, is to introduce methods for uncovering barriers and benefits.

FOUR STEPS FOR UNCOVERING BARRIERS AND BENEFITS

Uncovering barriers and benefits involves four steps. 1) Begin by reviewing relevant articles and reports. 2) Following this review, carry out observations of people engaging in the behavior you wish to promote (e.g., biking to work) as well as the behavior that you wish to dissuade people from participating in (e.g., driving to work). 3) Conduct focus groups to explore in-depth attitudes and behaviors of your target audience regarding the activities you wish to encourage and discourage. 4) Building on the information obtained from the focus groups, conduct a survey with a random sample of your target audience. A survey can enhance knowledge of the barriers to the behavior you wish to promote as well as what would precipitate action.

If you have a consultant doing this research for you, it is wise to ask for an interim report at the end of these four steps, in which information gleaned from the literature review is presented; results of the observations, focus groups and survey are detailed; and promising social marketing strategies based on this research are identified. For organizations that typically have research undertaken by consultants, this chapter is meant to provide information against which you can assess their work. If you are likely to do this work internally, this chapter will provide you with enough information to define a clear research strategy. When combined with additional reading, this chapter will provide you with a template for conducting your research in-house.[1] Finally, if you have limited time and/or

CBSM WEBSITE

The *Fostering Sustainable Behavior* website (cbsm.com) has a treasure-trove of resources for uncovering research on barriers and benefits. The site has searchable databases of academic articles, reports and cases. In addition, the site includes discussion forums where you can seek information from program planners from around the globe as well as search past discussion threads.

budget for discovering barriers and benefits, this chapter concludes with suggestions for how to do this step quickly and inexpensively.

1. LITERATURE REVIEW

Since the barriers and benefits to sustainable behavior are often activity-specific (see the previous chapter for more information), the first step in designing a community-based social marketing strategy is to review relevant articles and reports. Prior to conducting your literature review, you should be clear on your mandate. If your position involves promoting the use of mass transit over driving to work, then your literature search is already well defined. However, if you have a broad mandate, such as promoting residential energy, you will need to further clarify your mandate before proceeding with your search. As noted in the previous chapter, residential energy conservation can include behaviors as diverse as weather-stripping, adding additional insulation to an attic, programing a thermostat, closing and opening windows, installing compact fluorescent bulbs, or planting trees.

There are four sources of information that you will want to include in your literature review.

▶ Thumb through trade magazines and newsletters for related articles. Often these articles are summaries of more extensive reports and can provide good leads for where to search for in-depth information.

▶ Discover what reports have been written on the topic by other agencies. These reports are often difficult to obtain but are well worth the effort. Begin by contacting organizations that act as information clearinghouses for the behavior you wish to promote. If a relevant clearinghouse does not exist, call several well-connected individuals to trace down reports that have been prepared for other organizations. In addition, search the reports database at the Fostering Sustainable Behavior website (cbsm.com) and post requests for barrier and benefit research to the site's discussion forums.

BE SPECIFIC

Prior to conducting barrier and benefit research you must first carefully select the behavior you are going to target. The behavior that you plan to research should be an end-state, non-divisible behavior. See the previous chapter for more information on selecting specific behaviors.

▸ Search the databases of your local university for related academic articles. Many of the articles that will be of interest to you can now be found online and are sometimes free. When you conduct these searches, pay particular attention to recent review articles that synthesize the current state of knowledge on the topic. Finally, at the Fostering Sustainable Behavior website (cbsm.com) you will find a searchable database of academic articles on fostering sustainable behavior. You can search this database by behavior and/ or the behavior change tools described in subsequent chapters.

▸ Once you have reviewed the reports and academic articles that you have found, call the authors of studies that are of particular interest. Often these individuals will have pre-press publications that you will not be able to find elsewhere. In addition, they may be currently engaged in research that can further inform your efforts. Academics can be a particularly useful resource for tracking down research articles and reports that you may have missed in your previous searches. Mention the studies you have found and ask if there are other studies that you should be aware of. They may well be willing to email you a listing of relevant articles. Finally, ask if you can call back at a later point in your project to obtain further advice. Cultivating a good relationship with an academic who works in your area can assist you not only with keeping abreast of current literature, but also with issues related to analyzing your barrier and benefit research and designing and evaluating your project.

Finally, if you are having the literature search done by consultants, ask that they search for relevant information in each of these four areas.

2. OBSERVATIONS

A surprising amount can be learned by simply observing who engages in the behavior you wish to promote and who doesn't. For instance, imagine that you are interested in delivering programs to encourage active lifestyles that also reduce CO_2 emissions. More specifically, you would like to encourage more elementary school children to walk and bike to school. You decide to begin by observing how children presently travel to school. In conducting these observations, you quickly learn that the majority of young children who bike and walk to school live within a short distance of their school and that their route to school does not involve having to cross major roads. You further notice that children from less affluent neighborhoods are more likely to walk or bike to school than children from more affluent areas. These easily obtained observations suggest potentially important barriers to active transportation as well as what neighborhoods may be most important to target. These observations, by themselves, are not a sufficient basis upon which to develop a program, but along with the literature review they can assist you in developing the questions that you will ask in both your focus groups and your survey. Here are some items to consider in doing observations:

▸ Only conduct observations if you can observe the behavior unobtrusively. In other words, your observations cannot be influencing the behavior of those you are watching. Note that while you may not be able to observe the end-state behavior unobtrusively, for example, the installation of a high efficiency shower head, you may be able to observe actions that precede it, such as the purchase of a shower head in a hardware store. If you are able to observe the purchase of an item, note the advice, if any, provided by store personnel. Do they, for example, note the energy and water efficiency advantages of some items over others? You might also note the length of time involved in making the decision, along with the price of the item and where it is placed in the store relative to competing products.

▸ Observe both those who are engaging in the behavior to be promoted and those that are engaged in the competing behavior to enhance your understanding of how these two groups differ.

▸ When possible, have two or three people independently observe the same behaviors. Their recorded observations should be very similar.

► Cease doing observations when you are no longer learning anything new.

When observed closely, many sustainable behaviors are actually comprised of clusters of sub-actions that make up the sustainable behavior. For example, composting involves two of these clusters. First, someone has to purchase a composter, put it together and then site it in their yard. Second, they have to find a container in which to store their kitchen organics, begin to place their organics in this container, repeatedly take the container out to their backyard composter, mix yard waste in with the kitchen organics, stir the composter occasionally, and, finally, harvest the compost and then begin the process again. Observations can assist not only in identifying these sub-actions, but also in beginning to identify their barriers. Note that for behaviors that are made up of sub-actions, a significant barrier to any one of the sub-actions may be sufficient to have someone cease engaging in the behavior. Consider the example with which I began this book with. It was no more difficult for my wife and me to collect organics in our kitchen in the winter than it was in the summer. However, it was the sub-action of taking the organics out to the composter in the winter that caused us to compost only seasonally. Exploring the barriers to sub-actions is one of the most important steps you can take in identifying barriers and benefits.

EXPLORE BEHAVIOR

Many sustainable behaviors are actually made up of clusters of sub-actions. Explore the barriers to these sub-actions to understand better the barriers to the behavior you wish to promote.

3. FOCUS GROUPS

The literature review and observations will assist in identifying issues to be explored further through focus groups. A focus group consists of six to eight individuals who have been paid to discuss issues that your literature review and observations have identified as important. It should be noted that when focus group participants are volunteers there is a strong likelihood that they are participating because they have a greater interest in the topic than others in your target audience. The participants for the focus groups are usually randomly chosen from your target audience. To select the participants, simply choose random phone numbers from the phone book if your project will be targeting the local community, or from a listing of organizations if your program is targeting commercial or agricultural sectors. When contacting the potential participants, be sure to let them know how they were selected. To ensure a good rate of participation, make it convenient for people to participate. Arranging transportation and childcare, when necessary, can significantly increase participation rates. Remember, you want your focus group participants to be as representative of your target audience as possible. The more barriers that you remove to participating, the more representative your focus groups will be.

Focus groups provide an opportunity to discuss in detail the perceptions and present behaviors of your target audience that are relevant to the activity you plan to promote. To maximize what you can learn from the focus group, you should come to the meeting with a set of clearly-defined questions that have been informed by your literature review and observations. Furthermore, you should place those that are already engaging in the behavior in one set of focus groups, and those that are not yet engaged in another set. Mixing those that active and inactive in the same focus groups can significantly affect the quality of information that you receive from those who are inactive. When someone is not yet engaging in a behavior, such as biking to work, they can feel quite uncomfortable participating in a focus group with others who are.

To begin the session you will want to inform participants that they were chosen at random to provide your organization with information about the relevant behavior. You should also reassure them that there are no right or wrong answers for the questions that you will be asking them and that what you are most interested in is their perceptions. You will also want to remind them that their responses are confidential. Since you will be steering the conversation through the set of questions you have created, you should have a co-worker act as a note taker.

As the facilitator for the discussion, it is important that you establish a supportive, but firm, role with the attendees. It is not unusual to have one or two members of a focus group attempt to monopolize the discussion and in so doing make other members feel that their comments are not important. Your role is to facilitate in such a way that less assertive members, or individuals who might have differing views, feel comfortable in speaking out. Prior to

REDUCING BIAS

Most people feel that they should act to protect the environment, even if they are inactive. This belief can lead inactive focus group participants to want to *present* themselves in the best environmental light possible. To counter this bias, begin the inactive focus groups by explaining that they have been selected specifically because they are inactive. Further, explain that the most helpful thing that they can do is provide you with frank information regarding what impedes them from acting and what would motivate them to act. By framing the conversation in this way, you can often overcome their desire to present themselves as environmentally concerned and active and have them focus instead on assisting you by being frank and honest.

conducting your first focus group you will need to be comfortable with statements such as, "I have received some very informative feedback from you, now I would like to hear what others have to say," or "I understand that you feel strongly about this issue, but I also know that some people have very different views on this matter, would anyone like to share them?" These statements assure participants that, even if there are some belligerent or overly-talkative members, you are ensuring that other members' views will be heard.

You should also remember that you are interested in people's views unadulterated by any information that you might present in your subsequent program. Therefore, avoid sending information packages prior to conducting focus groups, though handing them out afterward is fine. If you provide information prior to running the focus groups, your participants will no longer be representative of your target audience.

When the focus groups are completed, you will want to summarize the comments that have been made. One effective technique is to tabulate the number of times that a specific comment was made, or agreed with, by members of the focus group. In general, you should pay close attention to comments that are made frequently, for example, "I would bike to work, if our roadways had protected lane ways that were just for cyclists."

4. SURVEY

Focus groups are an essential step in enhancing your understanding of how community residents view the behavior you wish to promote. However, by themselves, focus groups do not always provide sufficient information to develop a community-based social marketing plan. Focus groups are limited by the small number of participants, the impact that members of the focus group have upon one another, and the qualitative nature of the answers obtained. The small number of participants makes generalizing the results to the larger community unwise and, while interviewing participants in groups is cost-effective, members of a focus group can have a substantial effect on what opinions are expressed. Furthermore, the qualitative data obtained in focus groups places limits on the types of analyses that can be performed. Despite these limitations, focus groups provide valuable in-depth information about what issues participants see as important and also how they speak about the topic (e.g., do they use the word watershed in speaking about local rivers and lakes?). As such, focus groups will help enrich your understanding of the activity you wish to promote, and help ensure that your survey will be well-constructed, comprehensive, and contain questions that will be readily understood by the respondents.

Several methods are available for obtaining reliable information on the current beliefs and behaviors of your target audience regarding the activity you wish to promote. These methods are person-to-person interviews, a mailed survey, and a phone survey. While personal interviews are capable of providing reliable and in-depth information, they suffer from two significant limitations—they are expensive to conduct and take a considerable amount of time to complete. To conduct person-to-person interviews, a random sample of your target audience would first be selected. Next, each of these potential participants would be mailed a letter introducing the purpose of the interview. Each would then be called and, if willing, a time for an interview would be arranged. Paid interviewers would then travel to each participant to conduct the interview. While this detailed process is occasionally warranted, conducting person-to-person interviews is usually an inefficient use of your resources.

In contrast, a mailed survey is much less expensive to conduct and the entire survey can be completed in a reasonable amount of time. However, mailed surveys have a major drawback—the number of people who will complete and return the survey, or what is referred to as the *response rate*, is often less than 10%. Such a low response rate brings into serious question the representative nature or *generalizability* of the findings. Given the inconvenience of completing and mailing the survey, individuals who participate are likely more interested in your topic than those who elect not to participate. As a result, participants in a mailed survey often provide an unrealistic picture of your target audience's attitudes and behavior.

Phone-based surveys have several advantages over mailed surveys and person-to-person interviews. First, compared with a mailed survey, it is possible to obtain a higher response rate, which will provide you with a more accurate assessment of attitudes and behavior. While it is possible to obtain a higher response rate, clearly not everyone will agree to participate. However, those individuals who choose not to participate can be asked to complete a brief refusal survey. A refusal survey consists of three to four questions that are also found in the complete survey, for example, does your household purchase green power? Further, the refusal survey normally takes no longer than half a minute to complete. Because the refusal survey is so brief, individuals who wish not to participate in the full survey frequently agree to complete the briefer refusal survey. By comparing responses of refusal-survey participants with those of full-survey participants, potential differences between participants and non-participants can be explored. If no differences exist between the two sets of responses, the results of the full survey can be more reliably generalized back to your target audience. If differences do appear, greater caution is warranted in generalizing the results. In addition to providing a higher response rate than a mailed survey, as well as the opportunity to conduct a refusal survey, phone surveys are less expensive to conduct than interviews and can be completed in a much shorter amount of time than person-to-person interviews.

Additional advantages of phone surveys include:

▶ Random-digit dialling of community residents is possible. This ensures a random sample of community residents;

▶ Phone access to otherwise difficult-to-reach populations is possible, for example, high rise apartments or rural households.

Phone surveys are relatively easy to staff and manage. Compared with personal interviews, fewer staff are needed, the staff need not be near the sample geographically, and supervision and quality control are easier. Note, however, that participation in phone surveys has been steadily dropping. In response to these declining participation rates, it would be worthwhile to see barrier and benefit research being taken on by federal agencies, such as the Australian Bureau of Statistics or Statistics Canada as these agencies often obtain high rates of participation.

INTERNET SURVEYS

Increasingly agencies are considering internet-based surveys as replacements for other forms of surveys. Before you consider using an internet-based survey, ask yourself whether your target audience is online? If a significant minority of your target audience is not online this is not an appropriate form of survey. To reduce costs, some survey firms are now soliciting participation over the phone and then if the participant is willing, having them complete the survey online.

SEVEN STEPS: SURVEY

Items to include in your survey will be guided by your literature review, observations, and focus groups. But how do you begin to write the survey? Writing a well-constructed survey takes time and patience. Use the following seven steps as guidelines to make that process easier.

STEP ONE: CLARIFY YOUR OBJECTIVE

Begin by writing a simple paragraph that describes what the survey is meant to accomplish. This paragraph has two purposes. First, it will force you to be clear on what the survey is to measure. Second, once you have it completed, you can show it to others involved in the project. You will be spending considerable time writing, conducting and analyzing the data from the survey, so you will want to make sure, from the outset, that those who have a stake in the results are all onboard regarding what the survey is to accomplish.

Imagine that you are designing a community-based social marketing strategy for composting. You have two purposes: 1) To encourage people who are presently not composting to begin; and 2) To encourage seasonal composters to compost throughout the year. Given this background, your objective statement might read something like this:

Sample Objective Statement:

This survey's primary purpose is to determine which factors distinguish year-round composters from individuals who never compost. A secondary purpose is to determine which factors distinguish year-round composters from seasonal composters.

Note that the objective paragraph for the survey indicates that there are two purposes—one of which is more important than the other. Giving priorities to different survey objectives can assist you later in deciding how many questions to devote to each task that the survey is to perform. It should also be noted that comparisons between three groups are required: year-round composters; non-composters; and seasonal composters.

STEP TWO: LIST ITEMS TO BE MEASURED

Once you are happy with your "survey objective statement," the next step is to create a list of items that "might" be included in the survey. Note that at this time you are not concerning yourself with writing questions, only with determining the "themes" that will be covered in the questionnaire. Most of the items on your list should come from what you have learned from your literature review, observations and focus groups. Once you have created a comprehensive list, organize it into logical groupings. Place items related to behavior together, group items related to attitudes together and, similarly, group demographic topics. Finally, once you have grouped the items on your list, you are ready to check each item against your "survey objective paragraph." For each item on your list you want to determine if it furthers the purpose of your survey. In other words, does it help to determine any of the goals laid out in your objective statement? If it doesn't, it should be eliminated. When you have your list finalized, you are ready to begin writing the survey.

STEP THREE: WRITE THE SURVEY

In writing the survey, you will want most, if not all, of your questions to be closed-ended. The answers to open-ended questions are difficult to analyze and greatly extend the length of your survey. Keep in mind that you will want respondents to be able to complete the whole survey in 10 minutes or less. To be able to ask as many questions as possible in a short amount of time, you will want to use only a few types of scales in your survey.

Six or seven-point scales are preferable to three-, four- or five-point scales, as they allow for a broader range of answers. Having a broader range is important, if most people are likely to be clustered at one end of the scale or the other. It is likely, for example, that if asked how frequently they recycle glass and food cans on a four point scale most people would respond with a "3" or "4". However, when the scale is expanded to six items, answers will be more dispersed. Whether you use a six- or seven-point scale will depend upon whether you wish to provide respondents with a midpoint. Using an odd-numbered scale provides a midpoint that allows respondents who are divided as to how to respond to select this option. However, the midpoint may also be selected by respondents who are unsure of how to answer. Whichever option you select, stay with it throughout the survey to avoid confusion for respondents.

Note also that only the endpoints should be spelled out for each scale (e.g., "1=never" and "6=all the time"). Providing just the endpoints reduces the length of time it takes to read the survey to the participants. Furthermore, it allows you to assume that the distance between each of the items on the scale (e.g., 4 to 5) is equal. If you provide labels for each of the items on the scale, the respondent can no longer infer that the distance between each of the items is equivalent. For example, we understand that the distance between 5 and 6 is equal to the distance between 4 and 5. However, we can't assume equivalence with labels (e.g., Is the distance between "6-strongly agree" and "5-moderately agree" the same as the distance between "5-moderately agree" and "4-mildly agree"?). Because the distance between the scale items is no longer equivalent when you apply labels, there are more limitations placed on how you can analyze the data subsequently.

Make sure that instructions to the surveyor are typed in capital letters to distinguish them from what is to be read to the respondent. You should not have to write the whole survey yourself. You may wish to include questions that were part of other surveys (just seek permission before doing so).

Remember, you can use the demographics items in other surveys as guides for your demographic section. Finally, as you write your survey, Fowler notes that you will want to ask four questions of each question in your survey:[2]

1. Is this a question that can be asked exactly as written?

2. Is this a question that will mean the same thing to everyone?

3. Is this a question that people can answer?

4. Is this a question that people will be willing to answer?

STEP FOUR: PILOT THE SURVEY

Once the survey has been written, pilot it with 10 to 15 residents. During the pilot, the wording and order of questions in the survey can be scrutinized. Questions that respondents find confusing or difficult to answer can be rewritten before the full survey is conducted. The pilot also ensures that each survey can be conducted in under 10 minutes. Miscalculations regarding the length of time that it takes to contact respondents or complete the survey can be very costly when it comes time to conduct the survey. Your pilot will help you to ascertain if your budget is realistic. Do not include the data you obtain from the pilot with the data you obtain from the actual survey.

STEP FIVE: SELECT THE SAMPLE

Once you have completed the pilot and made whatever revisions are necessary, you are ready to obtain your sample. At this point you have two options. First, you may decide to have the survey completed by a survey research firm. You will likely be quoted a price per survey that will include all charges, including conducting the survey, the refusal survey, and entering the data into a software program for data analysis.

If you decide to conduct the survey yourself, and your target audience is residential, you may wish to have a firm provide you with a list of randomly derived residential phone numbers for your community. How many people should you sample? There is no easy answer to this question and here is where cultivating a good relationship with an academic working in the field can be of assistance. The size of the sample and how it is obtained will determine how confident you can be in your results. However, there is one other issue that will determine the sample size needed. Certain types of statistical analyses require a minimum number of participants for each barrier investigated (often 10 to 15) and often an equal number of individuals who are active and inactive on the activity you wish to promote.

STEP SIX: CONDUCT THE SURVEY

Complete the survey as quickly as possible to reduce the likelihood that some real-world event coincides with it. For example, imagine that you were conducting a survey on pollution and wildlife just as the BP oil rig in the Gulf of Mexico began spewing oil.

STEP SEVEN: ANALYZE THE DATA

Many of the current statistical packages, such as the Statistical Package for the Social Sciences (SPSS) make analyzing data much easier than it was even a few years ago. Obtaining descriptive statistics, frequencies, and comparing means is now as simple as pulling down a menu and selecting the variables and analysis that you want. Gone are the days when you had to write complex computer instructions to analyze data. The result is that basic statistics are now within reach of virtually everyone. However, you will want to go beyond obtaining the means and frequencies to lay the groundwork for your community-based social marketing campaign.

If you glance back at the survey objective statement, you will notice that the survey had two purposes: distinguishing between composters and non-composters, and distinguishing between year-round composters and those who compost seasonally. To answer these two questions requires multivariate statistics such as multiple regression, discriminant analysis or logistic regression. Multivariate statistics allow you to determine the factors that distinguish householders who compost from those who do not, and also enables you to analyze the relative importance of these factors. For example, in a study that I conducted with a former student, we used discriminant analysis and revealed the following five factors were most important in distinguishing year-round composters from non-composters.[3] Note that these factors are presented in order of importance:

▶ Those who composted reported a greater desire to reduce the amount of waste they produced than did non-composters.

▶ Non-composters perceived composting to be a more unpleasant activity than those who composted (e.g., they associated it with unpleasant odors, flies, rodents).

▶ Composters perceived the activity to be more convenient than did those who did not compost.

▶ Those who did not compost believed that they did not have the time to compost.

▶ Composting households reported recycling glass and cans more frequently.

Knowing which factors are most important in distinguishing individuals who have adopted a sustainable behavior from those who have not is an essential step in developing a community-based social marketing strategy. The results above provide a clear indication of some of the barriers that would need to be surmounted to encourage more people to compost. For example, perceptions that composting is unpleasant, inconvenient and involves a significant investment of time are important issues that a community-based social marketing strategy would need to address.

Analyzing the data using multivariate statistical techniques is an essential aspect in the development of a sound marketing strategy. Less sophisticated statistical approaches, such as calculating means or correlations, are limited in their ability to provide information on the relative importance of the factors that lead individuals to engage in the behaviors of interest to you. Unless you or someone else in your organization has a background in statistics, you will want to obtain assistance at this point. Many graduate students are trained in multivariate statistics and with a few phone calls you should be able to find someone who will do your analyses for you. Don't be daunted at this point. While the statistical techniques that are needed require someone who is statistically sophisticated the results of these analyses can be presented in a straight-forward, understandable format as can be seen above.

WHEN YOU HAVE LITTLE TIME, MONEY OR BOTH

It is tempting to skip barrier and benefit identification when you have limited time or financial resources. While the temptation is understandable, failing to conduct barrier and benefit research dramatically reduces the likelihood that your program will be successful. Rather than skipping this step, do the following to obtain useful information regarding barriers and benefits.

▶ Conduct a literature search as it can be done quickly and inexpensively.

▶ Carry out observations of those who are engaged in the behavior you wish to promote and those who are not. Observations can also be carried out quickly and inexpensively.

▶ Replace the focus groups and survey with intercept surveys. An intercept survey involves asking two simple questions of representatives of your target audience: "What makes it difficult or challenging for you to do 'X'?" and "What do you see as beneficial or rewarding about doing 'X'?" Go to locations where you target audience congregates. For example, if the topic of interest is reducing the transfer of aquatic invasive species from one watershed to another, then boat launches and marinas would be good locations to ask these questions. Ask people if you can have a moment of their time to ask them two questions. You should pose these two questions both to people who are engaged in the behavior to be promoted and those that are not. Make sure that you carry out these intercept surveys in a variety of locations to ensure greater representativeness. Finally, tabulate your responses to reveal how these two groups differ.

Conducting a literature search, observations, and intercept surveys might be done in as little as a week and can provide you with a firm foundation for developing a community-based social marketing strategy.

INTERCEPT SURVEYS

When you have little time or finances, replace the focus groups and survey with an intercept survey. Intercept surveys can be done quickly and inexpensively and can provide you with a more solid information upon which to develop your community-based social marketing strategy.

SOME CLOSING THOUGHTS

Identifying barriers is an essential first step in designing a successful program. While significant pressures exist to skip this step, the simple truth is that it is impossible to design an effective strategy without identifying barriers and benefits. In my experience, the four most common reasons for skipping barrier and benefit identification include:

▸ Belief that the barriers to the activity are already known;

▸ Time constraints;

▸ Financial constraints;

▸ Managerial staff who do not support conducting preliminary research.

BELIEFS & BARRIERS

Anecdotal beliefs regarding why people do or do not engage in a sustainable behavior can be tenaciously held. Once these beliefs exist we tend to look for information that confirms our beliefs and disregard information that would discount them. As a consequence, be prepared for resistance to doing barrier and benefit research.

Preconceived notions about barriers and benefits to an activity are difficult to overcome. By our very nature we develop theories about why people behave as they do. If we didn't, we would find it very difficult to understand and interact with others. This tendency to develop theories about the behavior of others can lead to a strong sense of self-assurance that the barriers and benefits for an activity are already well understood. Research in social psychology convincingly demonstrates, however, that once we have developed a "hunch" we tend to pay attention to information that supports our view, and discount or disregard information that would contradict it. As a consequence, we can come to believe very strongly in our own personal theories, even though they may have no factual basis. To be an effective community-based social marketer requires a healthy dose of skepticism about your own and others' personal theories.

Conducting preliminary research to identify barriers and benefits takes time. In a well-organized project you can expect the identification of barriers to add two to four weeks to the development of a strategy (less if you use intercept surveys). However, the length of time required to identify barriers and benefits pales when compared to the time and effort involved in having to design and deliver a new program if the first is unsuccessful. Similarly, while identifying barriers and benefits adds to the expense of delivering a program, given the much greater likelihood of delivering a successful program there is a high return on investment.

Building support among managerial staff will often involve dealing directly with the concerns listed above. Time and cost issues can often be dealt with by noting, as discussed above, that identifying barriers and benefits will usually save both time and money by reducing the likelihood of having to mount multiple campaigns. Managers, like everyone else, develop theories about behavior and are just as prone to believe that they already know the barriers and benefits for the activity you are trying to promote. There is a strong likelihood that they may ascribe to the attitude-behavior or economic self-interest approaches discussed in the first chapter. These perspectives are, after all, widely accepted. Finally, arrange, if possible, for managerial staff to read this book or attend a workshop on community-based social marketing. This book has been widely read in Australia, Canada, New Zealand, the United Kingdom and the United States. In these countries workshops on community-based social marketing have been attended by a large number of managers. In fact, in these nations, community-based social marketing is being increasingly specified by management as the method by which programs *must* be delivered.

Once you have identified the barriers and benefits for a behavior you wish to promote, you will want to consider what strategies you can use to address them. The next chapter provides an overview of how to develop a community-based social marketing strategy. It is followed by a series of chapters which introduce behavior change tools that you can incorporate into the programs you design.

Step 3: Developing Strategies

> *There's no use talking about the problem unless you talk about the solution.*
>
> **Betty Williams**

If a behavior change program is to be effective, careful consideration needs to be given to strategy development. As noted previously, too often behavioral change programs are based on hunches rather than solid information regarding the barriers and benefits to a behavior. Furthermore, the methods that are utilized in these progams are frequently not based on best knowledge from the social sciences regarding how to facilitate changes in behavior. When programs are not based on a solid foundation, there is a much higher likelihood that either they will not change behavior or that changes that do occur are not as substantial as they might have been.

This chapter will briefly introduce how to design a community-based social marketing strategy. It is followed by seven chapters that introduce behavior change tools that you can incorporate into your programs. It is premature at this point to introduce how to use these tools, as they have not yet been presented. Instead, this chapter will provide an overview of how to design effective strategies. Following the behavior change tool chapters, we will revisit developing strategies and clarify how to use these tools effectively.

OVERVIEW

As the graphic below indicates, developing a community-based social marketing strategy involves addressing two behaviors simultaneously: 1) the behavior to be encouraged; and 2) the behavior to be discouraged. We want to reduce barriers and increase benefits for the behavior to be encouraged, while doing the reverse for the opposing behavior. Too frequently, environmental program planners focus solely on the behavior they wish to encourage without giving adequate thought to the opposing behavior. By also addressing the behavior to be discouraged, we can make the desired action more attractive in contrast. Two examples will clarify the importance of this two-pronged approach.

Imagine that you are creating a program to encourage bicycling as a means of commuting to work. If we were to focus just on encouraging biking, as many organizations do, we might create bike lanes to make biking safer, encourage having shower facilities at work places, and ensure that there are adequate locations for securely

HUMILITY

Developing effective community-based social marketing strategies involves a good deal of humility. Avoid the temptation to assume that you know what strategy will work. Instead, carefully explore the barriers and benefits to the behavior you wish to promote prior to considering what strategies might work.

Behavior	Barriers	Benefits
Enourage	⬇	⬆
Discourage	⬆	⬇

locking bikes. While each of these approaches reduces the barriers to biking, nevertheless many commuters might still see driving as more convenient. To alter these perceptions, we need to increase the barriers and reduce the benefits of driving. This might be accomplished in several ways, such as placing a carbon tax on gasoline, reducing available parking, increasing parking rates, altering the layout of streets to slow traffic, and introducing congestion charges as London, England has done. Each of these approaches discourages driving and makes bicycling, in contrast, more attractive.

A similar approach can be used for increasing the adoption of lawn-care practices that do not involve pesticide use. The traditional approach has been to educate householders about these alternative practices. While some residents will adopt these practices simply based on learning about them, much higher levels of adoption can be reached if we simultaneously address the alternative behavior that we wish to discourage, pesticide use. As with car driving, there are multiple approaches that might be used. These include passing a law that individuals purchasing pesticides for residential use must have taken a course on their safe use, or requiring that manufacturers add a dye to pesticides which turns a lawn bright red until the pesticide is no longer present. Once again, by simultaneously focusing on both the behaviors to be encouraged and discouraged, we have a much higher probability of seeing the desired behavior adopted.

DEVELOPING STRATEGY PRINCIPLES
Developing an effective community-based social marketing strategy is predicated on first having carefully selected an end-state, non-divisible behavior, and then having identified and prioritized its barriers and benefits. By following the methods outlined in the previous chapter, not only will you have identified a number of barriers and benefits, but will likely also know which of these barriers and benefits are most important. Knowing which barriers and benefits are most important will allow you to focus your limited resources.

1. **SELECT TOOLS BASED ON BARRIERS AND BENEFITS:** To design an effective strategy, select tools that are tailored to the barriers and benefits you identify. For example, if lack of motivation is a barrier, you might consider the use of commitment, social norms or incentives—each of which are described in the following chapters.

2. **SCRUTINIZE YOUR DESIGN WITH FOCUS GROUPS:** Prior to piloting your strategy, conduct focus groups to receive feedback on your proposed strategy. If the strategy receives positive reviews, you are ready to pilot. If not, you will want to make further refinements.

3. **PILOT TEST YOUR STRATEGY:** In the pilot, you test the effectiveness of the strategy with a limited number of people. Essentially, you want to know, before committing to using the strategy throughout a community, that it will work effectively. If the pilot is successful, you can be much more confident of success when you broadly implement the strategy. If the pilot is unsuccessful, then you need to make further revisions, and pilot again before broad-scale implementation and evaluation.

As can be seen above, the design of a community-based social marketing strategy is pragmatic; each step builds on those that precede it. Effective design will not only help ensure the success of a program, but can also serve one other important purpose; cementing funding support. Increasingly, funding agencies are demanding that projects have a solid research foundation and are piloted before being implemented. The process briefly introduced in this chapter, and expanded upon following the behavior change chapters, can help you to persuade agencies that your initiative is worth supporting.

Commitment: From Good Intentions to Action

> " *Our deeds determine us as much*
> *as we determine our deeds.*
>
> **George Elliot**

Imagine being asked to place a large, ugly, obtrusive billboard with the wording "DRIVE CAREFULLY" on your front lawn. When a researcher, posing as a volunteer, made precisely this request, numerous residents in a Californian neighborhood flatly declined.[1] That they declined is hardly surprising, especially since they were shown a picture of the billboard almost completely obscuring the view of another house. What is surprising, however, is that fully 76% of another group of residents in this study agreed to have the sign placed on their lawn. Why would over three-fourths of one group agree, while virtually everyone in the other group sensibly declined? The answer lies in something that happened to the second group prior to this outlandish request being made. The residents who agreed in droves to have this aberration placed on their lawn were previously asked if they would display in the windows of their cars or homes a small, three inch sign that said, "BE A SAFE DRIVER." This request was so innocuous that virtually everyone agreed to it. Agreeing to this trivial request, however, greatly increased the likelihood that they would subsequently consent to having the billboard placed on their lawn.

Are these findings a mere anomaly? Apparently not. In another study, a researcher, identifying himself as a member of a consumer group, called and asked householders if he could ask them a few questions about their soap preferences.[2] A few days later the same researcher called back asking for a much larger favor, "Could I send five or six people through your house to obtain an inventory of all the products in the house?" The caller carefully explained that this "inventory" would require searching through all of their drawers and closets, etc. Having agreed to the smaller request only a few days earlier, many of the householders apparently felt compelled to agree with this much larger and more invasive request. Indeed, over 50% agreed, more than twice as many relative to householders who had not received the prior request. These surprising findings have now been replicated in a variety of settings. In each case, individuals who agreed to a small initial request were far more likely to agree to a subsequent larger request. For example:

▶ When asked if they would financially support a recreational facility for the handicapped, 92% made a donation if they had previously signed a petition in favor of the facility, compared with 53% for those who had not been asked to sign the petition.[3]

▶ Residents of Bloomington, Indiana, were called and asked if they would consider, hypothetically, spending three hours working as a volunteer collecting money for the American Cancer Society. When these individuals were called back three days later by a different individual, they were far more likely to volunteer than another group of residents who had not been asked the initial question (31% versus 4%, respectively).[4]

▶ A sample of registered voters were approached one day prior to a U.S. presidential election and asked, "Do you expect you will vote or not?" All agreed that they would vote. Compared to voters who were not asked this simple question, their likelihood of voting increased by 41%.[5]

▸ Ending a blood-drive telephone call with the query, "We'll count on seeing you then, OK?" increased the likelihood of individuals showing up from 62% to 81%.[6]

▸ Individuals who were asked to wear a lapel pin publicizing the Canadian Cancer Society were nearly twice as likely to subsequently donate than were those who were not asked to wear the pin.[7]

▸ When residents of a college community were asked to sign promise cards to use crosswalks and yield to pedestrians in crosswalks when driving, crosswalk usage increased by 10% and yielding to pedestrians in crosswalks increased by 21%.[8]

UNDERSTANDING COMMITMENT

Why does agreeing to a small request lead people to agree subsequently to a much larger one? When individuals agree to a small request, it often alters the way they perceive themselves. That is, when they sign a petition favoring the building of a new facility for the handicapped, the act of signing subtly alters their attitudes on the topic.[9,10] Through a process that Darryl Bem refers to as *self-perception* they come to view themselves as the type of person who supports initiatives for the handicapped.[11] When asked later to comply with the larger request, giving a donation, there is strong internal pressure to behave "consistently." Similarly, saying that you "think" you would volunteer for the Cancer Society, vote in an election, give blood or wear a lapel pin, alters your attitudes and increases the likelihood that you will later act in a way that is consistent with your new attitudes.

Consistency is an important character trait.[12] Those who behave inconsistently are often perceived as untrustworthy and unreliable. In contrast, individuals whose deeds match their words are viewed as being honest and having integrity. The need in all of us to behave consistently is underscored by an intriguing study on a New York City beach. In this study, a researcher posing as a sunbather put a

SELF PERCEPTION

Self-Perception Theory intriguingly suggests that if we can provide opportunities for people to engage in sustainable behaviors conveniently, the very act of engaging in those behaviors will shape their attitudes. For example, prior to curbside recycling being introduced, most individuals had no strongly held beliefs regarding the importance of waste reduction. However, when these same individuals received their new curbside containers and began to recycle, their participation in recycling led them to come to view themselves as the type of person who believed that waste reduction was important. This process suggests that we should look for occasions to provide people with the opportunity to engage in actions, that upon reflection, alter their beliefs. Furthermore, it is likely these beliefs will be most strongly held when the opportunity exists to engage in these actions frequently. For example, recycling or turning off a vehicle engine or computer equipment, are all repetitive actions which should lead those that engage in them to more strongly believe in the importance of reducing waste and emissions.

blanket down some five feet from a randomly selected sunbather. He then proceeded to relax on the blanket for a few minutes while listening to his radio. When he got up he said to the person beside him, "Excuse me, I'm here alone and have no matches ... do you have a light?" He then went for a walk on the beach, leaving the blanket and radio behind. Shortly afterwards, another researcher, posing as a thief, stole the radio and fled down the beach. Under these circumstances, the thief was pursued 4 times out of 20 stagings. However, the results were dramatically different when the researcher made a modest request prior to taking the walk. When he asked the person beside him to "watch his things," in 19 out of the 20 stagings the individual leapt up to pursue the thief. When they caught him some restrained him, others grabbed the radio back, while yet others demanded an explanation. Almost all acted consistently with what they had said they would do.[13]

The need to behave consistently is further supported by findings that a substantial amount of time can pass between the first and second request, and that the second request can be made by a different individual. That considerable time can pass between the two requests provides further evidence that complying with the initial request alters the way we see ourselves in an enduring way. Furthermore, that we will comply with a second request initiated by a new person, indicates that these changes are not transitory; otherwise we would only feel bound to comply if the second request were made by the same individual who had made the initial request.

COMMITMENT AND SUSTAINABLE BEHAVIOR

As detailed above, commitment techniques have been shown to be effective in promoting a diverse variety of behaviors. This behavior change tool has also been shown to be effective in promoting sustainable behavior. Here are several examples:

> ► In research carried out with Pacific Gas and Electric, home assessors were trained to make use of commitment strategies as well as other behavior change tools.[14] The assessors were trained to secure a verbal commitment from the householder. For example, the householder might be asked, "When do you think that you'll

LEARNING MORE

The fostering sustainable website (cbsm.com) includes searchable databases of academic articles, reports, cases, and discussion forums. To learn more about commitment, simply search these databases using "commitment" as the search term.

have the weather-stripping completed? ... I'll give you a call around then, just to see how it's coming along, and to see if you're having any problems." These subtle changes in how the assessment was presented resulted in substantial increases in the likelihood that householders would retrofit their homes. In fact, using these behavior change tools resulted in three to four times as many people electing to retrofit their homes.

► Commitment techniques have also been applied in the retail sector. In this study, small retail firms were randomly assigned to either a "mild commitment," "strong commitment" or "control" condition.[15] In the "mild commitment" condition, the names of the firms were published every other month along with information about the energy conservation initiative. In the "strong commitment" condition not only the names of the firms were published, but also the extent to which they had, or had not, saved energy. In all three cases, companies received information on steps they could take to reduce energy use and received a free energy audit. While the three groups did not differ in the amount of electricity they consumed, the two commitment conditions used significantly less natural gas than did the control group. Importantly, firms in the "mild commitment" condition used less natural gas than firms in the "strong commitment" condition. Informal comments from the owners of the companies in the "strong commitment" condition suggest that they felt trapped by the public disclosure of their initial lack of success in saving energy and that they subsequently stopped attempting to save energy. It is important to note that, in this study, there was no explicit commitment pledge. The researchers assumed that having their names publicly displayed would enhance commitment, but they did not directly ask for a commitment.

► Commitment has also been used to promote bus ridership. Individuals who did not ride the bus were assigned to one of four conditions. In the "information only" condition, participants received route and schedule information as well as identification cards that allowed ridership to be monitored. In the "commitment

USE "CALL BACKS"
One of the more useful strategies that you can build into your programs involves call backs. When a household or business expresses interest in engaging in a new behavior simply ask: "When do you think you will get around to that?" When the person responds, ask if they would like a phone call around that time to help troubleshoot any problems they might run into. If the individual says "yes," the likelihood that they will carry out the new behavior has likely risen dramatically. Agreeing to the phone call will mobilize them to act in anticipation of the call.

Canada's "Turn it Off" Campaign

Canadians idle their engines an average of eight minutes a day.[16] This unnecessary idling contributes to both climate change and poor air quality. To gauge the possibility of reducing engine idling, a pilot study was conducted in two locations in which idling is common: schools and Toronto Transit Commission "Kiss and Ride" parking lots. Idling occurs frequently at the end of the school day when parents and guardians are waiting to pick a child up. Idling is also common at Toronto's aptly named Kiss and Ride parking lots when partners are waiting at the end of the work day for a significant other to return on a train from downtown Toronto. In fact, baseline observations indicated that motorists in these two locations were idling their engines 53% of the time.

Two strategies to reduce engine idling were pilot tested. In the first strategy, a minimum of four signs were placed in various locations at the schools and Kiss and Ride parking lots. The signs were attached to concrete bases and were at a lower height than most signs in order to increase the probability that they would be seen. By themselves, the signs had no effect on engine idling.

Concurrent with the first strategy, a second strategy was tested in which the signs were used in conjunction with personal contact, prompts and commitment. The following script was used for these conversations:

© Natural Resources Canada

"Good afternoon/ evening. My name is _____ and I am working with the City of Toronto on a project aimed at reducing vehicle engine idling. We want to decrease the harmful emissions that occur when vehicle engines are left running.

These emissions, as you may know, decrease air quality and contribute to climate change. We are asking motorists to make a commitment to turn off their engine when they are parked and are waiting in their vehicle. Would you be willing to join the growing number of people who have made a similar pledge and agree to turn of your vehicle's engine when you are parked and waiting in your vehicle? We are asking people who make such a pledge to turn off their vehicle engine to place this sticker on their window. By doing so the sticker will both serve as a reminder to you to turn your engine off, and as a display of your commitment to reduce engine idling. The sticker has been designed so that it can be easily removed from your window at a later time. Would you be willing to attach this sticker to your window? We are also giving out these information cards which explain how turning off your engine can save you money, help you breathe easier and spare the air. Would you like to have one?"

While the signs by themselves did not reduce engine idling, when combined with personal contact and commitments, the frequency of engine idling was reduced by 32% and idling duration by 73%. These remarkable reductions occurred despite the fact that each conversation lasted only about a minute per vehicle.[17]

The effectiveness of this pilot led Natural Resources Canada to create an anti-idling toolkit that could be utilized by municipalities across Canada. This toolkit included all the resources that a community or organization would need to launch their own anti-idling program. As a consequence of developing this toolkit and making it freely available on the web, over 200 Canadian communities have now delivered their own anti-idling programs.[18]

Perhaps the most important lesson from Natural Resources Canada's anti-idling program is the feasibility of following up a successful pilot with the development of toolkits that can be utilized by others. Given that similar barriers and benefits exist in other locations (a testable assumption), the development and dissemination of these toolkits could lead to the rapid deployment of successful programs in numerous communities. Given that many communities are facing the same challenges, the development of such toolkits should be a priority.

© *Natural Resources Canada*

condition," participants made a verbal pledge to ride the bus twice a week for four weeks, while in the "incentive condition," participants were given ten free bus tickets and were informed that they could receive more tickets when they had used the initial tickets. Finally, in the "combined condition," participants both made a pledge to ride twice a week for four weeks and received free tickets. Each of the three conditions increased bus ridership. However, it was found that participants in the "commitment only" condition rode the bus just as frequently as the participants in the "incentive condition" and the "combined condition." Importantly, these effects were observable during two follow-ups, conducted at three and twelve weeks after the intervention.

► In a unique study, homeowners were mailed either a shower flow restrictor along with a pamphlet on energy conservation or just the pamphlet alone.[19] Homes that received the shower flow restrictor in addition to the pamphlet were not only more likely to install the restrictor, an obvious finding, but were also more likely to engage in the other conservation actions mentioned in the pamphlet, for example, lowering the temperature on their water heaters, installing setback thermostats or cleaning their furnaces. Apparently, having installed the shower flow restrictor altered how these individuals perceived themselves. In short, they came to see themselves as the type of individuals who are concerned about energy conservation and, as a result, carried through with the other actions suggested in the pamphlet.

► Obtaining a signed commitment increased curbside recycling in Salt Lake City, Utah, more than receiving a flyer, a telephone call or personal contact alone.[20]

► Farmers in the Netherlands who received farm-specific information on the actions they could take to protect their local watershed and enhance biodiversity, and subsequently committed publicly to engage in these actions at a meeting, were more likely to alter their behavior than were farmers who received only farm-specific information.[21]

USING COMMITMENTS EFFECTIVELY

A variety of studies have clarified when commitments are likely to be most effective. Written commitments appear to be more effective than verbal commitments.[22] In a study that investigated the impact of verbal versus written commitments, households were assigned to one of three groups. In the first group, homes simply received a pamphlet underscoring the importance of recycling newspaper. In the second group, households made a verbal pledge to recycle newsprint. In the third group, households signed a statement in which they committed themselves to recycle newsprint. Initially, the households that made either a verbal or written commitment recycled more newsprint than households that received only a pamphlet. However, only the households that committed themselves by signing the statement were still recycling when a follow-up was conducted.

Whenever possible, ask permission to make a commitment public. The dramatic impact that public commitments can have is illustrated in a study in which either a private commitment to conserve electricity and natural gas was obtained, or a public commitment was obtained, in which names would be published in the local newspaper.

CHART: PUBLIC COMMITMENTS AND ENERGY USE

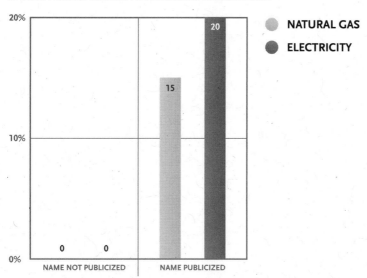

PUBLIC & DURABLE

Public and durable commitments enhance the likelihood
that the individual who made
the commitment will engage in
the behavior. However, because
the commitment is public, and
therefore can be witnessed by
others, these commitments also
foster social norms and social
diffusion, which are discussed in
subsequent chapters.

Those who agreed to a public commitment saved significantly more energy than did householders who were in the private condition. Even after the researchers informed the participants who had agreed to a public commitment that their names would not be published, they continued to save energy. While the names were never publicized, simply asking for this permission brought about a 15% reduction in natural gas used and a 20% reduction in electricity used. Importantly, these reductions were still observable 12 months later.[23] Public commitments are likely so effective because of our desire to be consistent. In short, the more public a commitment, the more likely we are to honor it.

Seeking commitments in groups can also be effective. When the economic and environmental benefits of recycling were explained to members of a retirement home, and they were asked to make a group commitment, there was a 47% increase in the amount of paper recycled.[24] The authors suggest that group commitments are likely to be effective in settings where there is good group cohesion. This suggests group commitments are likely to be effective in well-established groups in which individuals care how they are viewed by other members of the group.

Commitment can be increased not only by seeking a verbal or written pledge, but also by actively involving the person. In the Pacific Gas and Electric study mentioned above, home assessors were trained to involve the home owner actively in the assessment.[25] Home owners were asked, for example, to peer into their attic to inspect the insulation level or to place their hand on an uninsulated water heater, etc. After being involved in this way, home owners are more likely to see themselves as committed to energy conservation.

Commitment strategies have been criticized as too labor-intensive to warrant implementation on a broad scale.[26] However, implementing commitment as part of a home visit, as was done in the Pacific Gas and Electric study, is a viable option. Furthermore, asking for a commitment when a service is provided, such as delivery of a compost unit or a water efficiency kit, is a natural opportunity to employ this strategy. Two other strategies are worth considering in making use of commitment. First, existing volunteer groups can be used. In one study, Boy Scouts asked residents to sign a statement agreeing to participate in a community recycling program. Those households who were asked to sign the statement were much more likely to participate than was a control group who was not asked (42% and 11%, respectively).[27]

Second, commitment strategies have also been shown to be effective when community "block leaders" implement them. A block leader is a community resident who already engages in the behavior that is being promoted and who agrees to speak to other people in their immediate community to help them get started. In this study, block leaders approached homes and used a variety of community-based social marketing strategies, including seeking a verbal commitment, to encourage the household to begin recycling. The homes that were visited by a block leader were more than twice as likely to recycle than was a group who received flyers.[28]

Commitments should be sought only for behaviors which people express interest in doing. Hence, if a block leader approaches a home and asks if the residents are interested in composting, commitment should only be sought if the household expresses an interest in the activity. Indeed, research suggests that commitment will not work if the person feels pressured to commit. In order for commitment to be effective, the commitment must be voluntary.

Earlier in this chapter I suggested that one of the reasons for the dramatic impact of small requests upon subsequent behavior was that responding to a small request alters how we see ourselves. If how we see ourselves is an important predictor of how we will act in the future, it makes sense that programs to promote sustainable behavior should actively assist people to see themselves as environmentally concerned. Support for this assertion comes from a study that investigated the impact of assisting people to see themselves as charitable.[29] In this study, householders were approached and asked if they would make a donation to the heart association. Half of the individuals who volunteered to make a donation were thanked and told, "You are a generous person. I wish more of the people I met were as charitable as you," while the other half were simply thanked. One to two weeks later these same individuals were approached by another individual and asked if they would donate money to Multiple Sclerosis. Not only did more of the "generously labeled" people give money to Multiple Sclerosis, they also gave more—fully 75% more. This research suggests that when possible we should be helping people to see themselves as environmentally concerned. For example, when encouraging someone to try a new activity, such as carpooling, we should begin by pointing out the other positive sustainable behaviors that they are already involved in.

A CHECKLIST FOR USING COMMITMENT

When considering using commitment, check that the following guidelines have been followed:

✓ Emphasize written over verbal commitments

✓ Ask for public commitments

✓ Seek group commitments

✓ Actively involve the person

✓ Consider cost-effective ways to obtain commitments

✓ Use existing points of contact to obtain commitments

✓ Help people to view themselves as environmentally concerned

✓ Don't use coercion (commitments must be freely volunteered)

✓ Combine commitment with other behavior change techniques

On the next page are a variety of examples of how commitments can be used to foster sustainable behavior.

Examples: Using Commitment to Foster Sustainable Behavior

Agriculture & Conservation

▶ As noted in this chapter, ask farmers to commit publicly at a meeting to engage in actions related to watershed and biodiversity protection.

▶ Protect nesting shore birds by asking beachgoers to keep dogs on a leash and to stay away from marked nesting areas. Make their commitments public and durable by requesting their picture be taken. Post the photos in displays along the boardwalks that lead to the beach. Posting the photos along these walkways serves as an ongoing reminder to these individuals of the commitment they have made each time they pass the display. Furthermore, the display serves as way of fostering social norms and social diffusion. (See the chapters on norms and social diffusion for more information.)

Energy

▶ As mentioned previously in this chapter, when conducting a home assessment, invite the home owners to participate.

▶ Conclude a home assessment visit by asking the home owners when they expect to complete activities such as weather-stripping or installing a programmable thermostat. Ask for permission to call back to help home owners troubleshoot any problems they had with installation. There is a high likelihood that they will engage in the action in anticipation of the call back.

Transportation

▸ Ask commuters to sign a public commitment that they will take mass transit once or twice a week for a specific period of time. (See the study on bus ridership in this chapter.)

▸ Ask vehicle owners to commit to turn their car off while waiting to pick someone up. Provide a prompt that they can affix to their windshield or dashboard to remind them to turn their engine off. (See the case study in this chapter for further information.)

▸ Ask car owners to commit publicly to checking their car's tire pressure once a month. Provide prompts at gas stations reminding people to check their tire pressure. Have gas attendants also commit to reminding people to check their tire pressure.

Waste & Pollution

▸ When distributing compost units, ask when the person expects to begin to use the unit and inquire if you can call shortly afterwards to see if he/she is having any difficulties.

▸ Ask households who have just received a compost unit to place a sticker on the side of their recycling container indicating that they also compost.

► Ask people entering grocery stores to wear a button or sticker supporting the purchase of products that have recycled content or are recyclable. (See also the chapter on social norms.)

► In retail outlets, place decals on household hazardous waste containers that provide information on where HHW can be taken for proper disposal. Partner with retail outlets to have customers sign the decal and commit themselves to taking unused amounts of the product to the depot for proper disposal.

 Water

► Ask homeowners to make a commitment to raise the height of their lawn mower, thereby reducing evaporation and the need for lawn watering.

Social Norms: Building Community Support

> *Belief, like any other moving body,*
> *follows the path of least resistance.*
>
> **Samuel Butler**

Imagine that you have agreed to participate in an experiment on visual discrimination. Upon arriving for the study, you are asked to take your place at a table at which five other participants are seated. As you take your seat, the experimenter explains that this study will involve making perceptual judgments regarding the lengths of four lines. He then projects an image on the screen at the front of the room. On the left side of the screen there is a line labelled "X." On the other side of the screen are three lines, labelled "A," "B" and "C." Your task, he explains, is a simple one: to select which of lines "A," "B" or "C" is equivalent in length to line "X." The experimenter then proceeds to show a variety of slides. For each slide, the other participants and yourself are asked to select the line that is equal to "X." After several slides, you are beginning to yawn and wonder how someone ever received a grant to conduct this research.

On the next slide, however, something unexpected happens. In response to the set of lines on the following page, the first

participant selects line "C" as the line
that is equal to "X." You rub your eyes
and look again. Yes, she did say "C"—
but clearly that is wrong, you think to
yourself. Your train of thought is broken
as the next participant also reports
that line "C" is equal to "X." After the
third, fourth, and fifth participants
also select "C," you begin to question

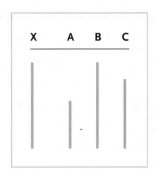

your own visual abilities, mentally make a note to have your eyes
checked and then utter what a moment ago was unthinkable. "Line C,"
you hear yourself saying, "is the correct choice."

When Solomon Asch conducted this study, approximately 75%
of the participants altered their answers at least once to concur with
the incorrect answers of others in the group, who, as you have by
now surmised, were accomplices of the experimenter.[1] Perhaps you
are thinking that these visual discriminations were difficult enough
to lead participants to question their selections. Unfortunately, they
were not. When participants were left on their own to select which of
the three lines was the correct match, the correct line was selected
99% of the time.

Asch's research is both surprising and troubling. In response
to the findings, he wrote, "That reasonably intelligent and well-
meaning young people are willing to call white black is a matter
of concern." Asch's findings are not unique, however. In a variety of
settings, people have been found to alter their answers to be in line
(no pun intended) with normative, though clearly incorrect, answers
given by others.

What is fascinating about Asch's study, and other research on
conformity, is that the tasks are often completely inconsequential.
In the larger scheme of things it simply doesn't matter which of the
lines is equal to "X." Nevertheless, people looked to the behavior of
those around them to determine how they would respond.

Asch's research underscores the important role that other people
have upon our own behavior. To date, however, too little attention
has been given to the significant impact that norms can have upon
the adoption of sustainable behavior. If we are to make the transition

to a sustainable future, it is critical that we are able to develop a set of societal norms that support sustainability. This chapter will introduce you to research which demonstrates the powerful influence that norms can have upon sustainable behavior, and provide guidelines for integrating the use of norms into the programs you deliver.

SOCIAL NORMS AND SUSTAINABLE BEHAVIOR

Several studies have documented the impact that social norms can have upon individuals engaging in sustainable behavior. At the University of California Santa Cruz's athletic complex, the male shower room has a sign that encourages that showers be turned off while users soap up.[2] More specifically, the sign reads: "Conserve water: 1. Wet down. 2. Water off. 3. Soap. 4. Rinse." This sign apparently had little effect on behavior. On average, only 6% of users were found to comply. One possibility was that people simply didn't see the sign. However, a survey of a random sample of students demonstrated that 93% were aware of the sign and its message.

Elliot Aronson and Michael O'Leary reasoned that students might be far more likely to comply with the sign if they observed another student following its instructions. To test this possibility, an accomplice entered the male shower room in the athletic complex, proceeded to the back of the room and turned on the shower. When another student entered, the accomplice turned off the shower, soaped up and then turned on the shower once more to rinse off. All of this was done with his back to the other student and without eye contact. When the accomplice modelled water conservation in this way, the percentage of students who turned off the shower to soap up shot up to 49%. Furthermore, when two accomplices modelled water conservation, the number of people who followed suit rose to 67%.

It is important to note that the changes in behavior observed in this study were not brought about by punitive measures. No "shower police" intervened if students did not turn off the shower while soaping up. It should be noted that two community-based social marketing strategies are employed in this study: prompts (the sign) and norms. While the sign by itself was ineffective in altering the behavior of those using the shower room, when it was combined with the norm, behavior changed dramatically.

LEARNING MORE

The Fostering Sustainable Behavior website (cbsm.com) includes searchable databases of academic articles, reports, cases, and discussion forums. To learn more about social norms, simply search these databases using "norms" as the search term.

The following study illustrates the importance of two types of norms: injunctive and descriptive. Injunctive norms provide information on what behaviors are approved or disapproved of, while descriptive norms indicate which behaviors are normally engaged in. Picture yourself leaving the local library and walking toward your car in the parking lot. As you get closer to your car, you notice that someone has left one of those annoying flyers not only under your windshield wipers, but everyone else's as well. You remove the flyer and crumple it up, but do you toss it on the ground? I am well aware that most of the people who will read this book will take the flyer home and put it in their recycling container, but what would most *other* people do in this situation? The answer, it turns out, depends upon what those around them do.

In a series of studies, Robert Cialdini and his colleagues placed flyers on every windshield in a library parking lot.[3] In one condition, as library patrons made their way back to their cars an accomplice walked past, picked up a littered bag and placed it in a garbage can. In the control condition, the accomplice simply walked past and did nothing. What impact did these simple acts have upon the library patrons? For those who observed the littered bag being picked up and thrown in the garbage (an injunctive norm), virtually no one littered the flyer. However, when the accomplice simply walked past and left the bag on the ground, over one-third threw the flyer on the ground! In a related study, Cialdini and his colleagues removed the injunctive norm of having an accomplice walk in front of the library patron and stop and pick up the garbage. In this follow-up study, they simply manipulated the number of flyers that were strewn about in the parking lot (descriptive norm). When the parking lot was littered with flyers, the library patrons littered as well. However, when only one flyer was littered in the parking lot, patrons littered significantly less. This research demonstrates the unique contributions that injunctive and descriptive norms can make to behavioral change. However, are there contexts in which we should be careful in using injunctive or descriptive norms?

USING NORMS EFFECTIVELY

The Iron Eyes Cody television ad is one of most highly regarded public service announcements (PSA) in the United States. Robert Cialdini notes that the ad was rated as one of the top television commercials of all time by *TV Guide*. It aired repeatedly in the 1970s and 1980s and garnered millions of dollars of free airtime.[4] Despite the widespread recognition that the PSA received, Cialdini suggests that the spot was likely not as effective as previously thought. The PSA showed a traditionally dressed American Indian canoeing along a river which is strewn with garbage. When he comes ashore he witnesses a bag of garbage thrown from a passing car. The spot finishes with a close up of his face with a tear rolling down his cheek.

Cialdini notes that the creators of this ad inadvertently placed injunctive and descriptive norms in competition with one another. In the PSA, the tear rolling down his cheek serves as an injunctive norm in which the act of littering is clearly disapproved of. However, the plethora of garbage through which he canoes serves as a descriptive norm, showcasing that many people litter. Over the last several years, several intriguing studies have investigated the impact that descriptive and injunctive norms can have upon sustainable behavior. Furthermore, they have shown why programs that utilize norms

The Ad Council, "People Start Pollution. People Can Stop It." © 1971, Keep America Beautiful, Inc.

have to be carefully constructed to avoid inadvertently encouraging a behavior we wish to discourage.

If an undesirable behavior, such as littering, is a frequent occurrence, showcasing the behavior may encourage others to engage in that action. For instance, in Arizona's Petrified National Forest, visitors have traditionally been greeted with signs that proclaim, "Your heritage is being vandalized every day by theft losses of petrified wood of 14 tons a year, mostly a small piece at a time." Unbeknownst to the park administration, the use of these signs was actually encouraging visitors to steal by displaying that many people in the past had taken home mementos.[5] Cialdini and his colleagues noted that the park administration had "stimulated

---

Increasing Hotel Towel Reuse

It is hard to stay at a hotel, any hotel, without seeing a card in the washroom admonishing us to reuse the towels. Most of these requests suggest that we do our part to protect the environment by reducing unnecessary laundering. However, are these appeals as effective as they could be in getting hotel patrons to reuse their towels?

To find out, Goldstein, Griskevicius and Cialdini conducted a simple, but elegant study.[6] Working with the management of a Phoenix-based hotel, they tested the efficacy of several different messages. The study compared the use of a standard environmental appeal, an appeal that made use of descriptive norms, and an appeal that made use of descriptive norms that were specific to the room the guest was staying in.

© Fedyaeva Maria, Shutterstock

the precise behavior they had hoped to suppress by making thievery appear commonplace—when, in fact, only 2% of the park's millions of visitors have every taken a piece of wood" (p. 8).[7] To investigate the impact that descriptive versus injunctive norms might have on the theft of petrified wood, they devised a study which involved alternating an injunctive and descriptive sign in three high-theft areas in the park. Each sign was used for an equivalent amount of time in each location. Similar to the sign that was already in use, the descriptive sign asked visitors not to steal the wood and showed several people stealing wood. In contrast, the injunctive sign also requested visitors not to take wood, but showed only one person doing so. What impact did the two signs have upon wood being

---

Below are the three messages that were used:

1. Environmental Protection: "HELP SAVE THE ENVIRONMENT. You can show your respect for nature and help save the environment by reusing your towels during your stay."

2. Descriptive Norm: "JOIN YOUR FELLOW GUESTS IN HELPING TO SAVE THE ENVIRONMENT. Almost 75% of guests who are asked to participate in our new resource savings program do help by using their towels more than once. You can join your fellow guests in this program to help save the environment by reusing your towels during your stay."

3. Room Specific Descriptive Norm: In contrast to the general descriptive norm, the room-specific descriptive norm replaced the sentence regarding reuse rates in the hotel with one specific to the very room. It read, "75% of the guests who stayed in this room (#xxx) participated in our new resource

saving program by using their towels more than once."

What impact did these different cards have upon towel use? When the standard environmental protection appeal was used, 37% of guests reused their towels. When the card referenced reuse figures for the hotel, the percentage increased to 44%. However, when the specific room that the guest was staying in was referred to, 49% reused their towels.

Goldstein and his colleagues suggest that we are most likely to be influenced by the behavior of those we perceive to be similar to ourselves. This research suggests that providing normative feedback on the behavior of similar others, such as colleagues in an office building, neighbors on a street, or other farmers in a watershed, may be particularly compelling in fostering behavioral changes.

stolen? When the descriptive sign, which depicted several people stealing wood was used, more than twice as many visitors stole wood from the park.[8]

In designing programs that make use of norms you need to carefully consider the possibility that providing descriptive information could actually decrease the desirable behavior amongst some individuals. This possibility has been carefully explored in several studies by Wes Schultz and his colleagues. In one study, households received information regarding energy conservation via door hangers.[9] Some households received information on their energy consumption along with information on whether their energy use was higher or lower than the neighborhood average (descriptive norms). In contrast, others received this same information along with a hand-written *smiling* emoticon if they used less than their neighbors and a *sad* emoticon if they used more (descriptive and injunctive norms combined). Interestingly, those households who received information that indicated that they were using more energy than their neighbors reduced their energy use. In contrast, those households who received information indicating that they were using less than their neighbors increased their energy use. However, when households who were using less than the neighborhood average were praised for their low use, they continued to use less energy.

Building on this research and approach, OPOWER has worked with utilities across the U.S. to provide descriptive and injunctive normative information regarding energy use. Households are provided with information on their energy use relative to other homes in their neighborhood. Over 1 million households presently receive normative feedback on their energy use and this feedback has been associated with a 2.4% reduction in residential energy use.[10,11]

For norms to be effective they need to be internalized by people. That is, people need to view the behavior which the norm prescribes as the way they "should" behave. Several studies demonstrate that it is possible to influence the acceptance of such norms. Joseph Hopper and Joyce McCarl Nielsen believe that an important motivation to recycle is the belief that it is simply the " right thing to do" (a social norm), despite the fact that it takes time and can be inconvenient. Further, they expect that this norm is most likely to develop through

CAREFUL USE

Descriptive norms can backfire if they make an undesirable behavior appear common. When an undesirable behavior is common, use injunctive rather than descriptive norms to address it. Further, providing descriptive information that showcases that an individual is doing better than average can lead that individual to do less well. To overcome this problem, combine descriptive information with praise (injunctive norms).

direct contact between people rather than through campaigns that rely upon prompts or information alone. To test these assumptions, the authors arranged for a sample of homes in Colorado to be divided into three groups.[12] In one group, households were visited by a volunteer block leader who spoke with them about curbside recycling, encouraged them to recycle, and then provided a reminder notice several days before the recycling collection date. In contrast, in the prompt group, households received a reminder notice a few days before the collection day, while in the information group households received a flyer that described the recycling program, indicated what items were acceptable and provided the collection dates. Those households who were visited by a volunteer block leader recycled nearly a third more often than households who received prompts and nearly three times as often as the homes who received the information flyer (further evidence of the ineffectiveness of information-based campaigns in bringing about behavior change). Not only were the volunteer block leaders most effective in altering behavior, but they alone had an impact upon norms. In comparing survey results from before and after this campaign, households who were visited by a block leader were more likely to report that they felt upset if they discarded recyclable materials and that they felt an obligation to recycle these materials. The prompt and information strategies had no impact upon these beliefs.

Many anti-littering campaigns have as their central message that littering is simply not acceptable behavior. When Oklahoma City initiated an anti-littering campaign, community norms regarding littering changed substantially. Prior to the campaign, 37% of the community indicated they would feel guilty if they littered. Two years following the campaign that figure had risen to 67%. The number of people who believed they would lose the respect of others if they littered nearly tripled in the same time period.[13]

Finally, normative strategies are likely to be particularly effective when people are being asked to change their behavior or adopt a different lifestyle. In these cases, behavioral research suggests that direct contact in which social norms, modelling (see chapter on effective communication), and social diffusion occur may be particularly important.[14]

A CHECKLIST FOR USING NORMS

Follow these guidelines in using norms:

✓ Make the norm noticeable.

✓ Present the norm at the time the targeted behavior is to occur. For example, upon entering a supermarket, customers could be greeted by a prominent display that indicates the percentage of shoppers who purposely select products that favor the environment.

✓ Use norms to encourage people to engage in positive behaviors (rather than only avoiding environmentally harmful actions).

✓ Be careful using descriptive norms when an undesirable behavior is common.

✓ Combine descriptive information with praise (injunctive norm) when someone is performing the sustainable behavior better than average.

Below are a variety of suggestions for using norms to promote sustainable behavior.

Examples: Using Norms to Foster Sustainable Behavior

Agriculture & Conservation

▸ Ask farmers who are committed to engaging in watershed and/or biodiversity protection for permission to install signs along the edge of their property showcasing the actions in which they are engaged. If possible, these signs should be placed in locations where they will be visible to the greatest number of other farmers (e.g., alongside the busiest highway).

Energy

▶ Attach gas mileage bumper stickers to very fuel-efficient cars.

▶ Attach decals to energy-efficient products in stores that indicate the number of people who believe it is important to purchase products that are more energy efficient.

 Transportation

▶ Provide information in the foyer of an organization regarding the percentage of staff who use mass transit, car pooling, walking or bicycling to get to work.

 Waste & Pollution

▶ Affix a decal to recycling container indicating "We Compost." See the chapter on social diffusion for an example of this sticker.

▶ Affix a decal to the recycling container indicating that the household buys recycled products.

▶ Ask supermarket shoppers to wear a button or sticker that shows their support for buying products that are recyclable or have recycled content (note that agreeing to wear a button or sticker also increases the likelihood that they will actually shop for these products).

 Water

▶ Publicly communicate the percentage of people who comply with municipal requests to restrict summer water use.

▶ Attach stickers to the sides of recycling containers showcasing that households have reduced either indoor and/or outdoor water use.

Social Diffusion: Speeding the Adoption of New Behaviors

> *Setting an example is not the main means of influencing another, it is the only means.*
>
> **Albert Einstein**

Think of the last book that you read, restaurant you ate at, or movie that you watched. What do each of these seemingly unrelated events have in common? All three were likely influenced by friends, family members, or colleagues. More important decisions, such as what neighborhood to live in, what school to send our children to, or who to have as a family doctor, are all similarly influenced.

Both the mundane and important decisions of our lives are strongly affected by a process known as *social diffusion* or *diffusion of innovations*.[1] In contrast with what nonpersonal sources of information, such as brochures or advertising, conversations that we have with others, and particularly with those whom we trust and perceive as similar to ourselves, have an inordinate influence.[2] While social diffusion has been studied and applied extensively in fields such as public health, it has received surprisingly little attention regarding sustainable behavior. This lack of application is striking as many sustainable behaviors, such as carpooling or installing a

73

grassed waterway on a farm, involve adopting a new innovation.[3] The relevance of social diffusion to the adoption of sustainable behaviors has been commented on by Aronson and Gonzales. They note that social diffusion can be easily observed by walking through California neighborhoods, where the homes that have installed solar collectors tend to "...'cluster' throughout the neighborhood— reflecting the social networks of residents who purchase and install solar heating devices" (p. 318).[4] I've witnessed this same process in the Pacific Northwest of the United States, where similar clusters of homes have replaced the grass in their front yard with drought-tolerant plants.

SOCIAL DIFFUSION AND SUSTAINABLE BEHAVIOR

Below are several examples of sustainable behaviors that have been influenced by social diffusion.

▸ During the 1930s, both American and Canadian farmers were losing dramatic amounts of topsoil from their fields. In response to this crisis, the U.S. government distributed brochures which detailed the problem and suggested actions, such as planting trees as wind screens, that could be taken to slow the loss of topsoil. Like the information campaigns discussed in the first chapter, this attempt to influence the behavior of farmers was a dismal failure. When it was clear that farmers were not changing their agricultural practices, the government tried a new approach that involved working directly with a small number of farmers. These farmers received direct assistance in adopting practices that would slow erosion. It was reasoned that farmers might be more apt to adopt new approaches if they were first modelled by a farmer in their area. Modelling a new technique, such as installing wind screens or alternative methods of tillage, it was believed, would be far more compelling than dryly describing the technique in a pamphlet. Further, it would encourage farmers to discuss the new technique and, if they observed that it was working successfully on a local farm, increase the likelihood that they would adopt it themselves. Unlike the campaign that involved distributing brochures, this approach was far more successful. Neighboring farmers observed the changes that the early adopters were making, discussed them with them, and adopted similar practices once they saw the results. As a consequence, these new agricultural practices diffused quickly.[5]

▶ Those who install programmable thermostats have been found to influence the likelihood of friends, family and coworkers installing them, but not their neighbors. This finding suggests the importance of social networks, over geographical proximity, in determining social diffusion.[6]

▶ Those who intend to install solar panels have been found to have friends and colleagues who had already installed them.[7]

▶ In a survey that investigated curbside recycling participation, recycling by friends and neighbors predicted recycling by the respondent.[8]

Whether a new sustainable behavior, or innovation, is likely to be adopted has been found to depend upon the following factors, which have been found to be highly predictive of social diffusion. [9,10,11,12]

▶ Relative Advantage: Is the behavior perceived to be clearly superior to the behavior it replaces?

▶ Perceived Risk: Will adopting the behavior increase the probability of financial loss or social disapproval?

▶ Complexity: Is the new behavior challenging?

▶ Compatibility: Is the behavior compatible with the values of the target audience?

▶ Trialability: Can the behavior be trialed, before making a long-term commitment?

▶ Observability: Is the behavior visible to others?

LEARNING MORE

To learn more about social diffusion, simply search the Fostering Sustainable Behavior website (cbsm.com) databases using "social diffusion" as the search term.

USING SOCIAL DIFFUSION EFFECTIVELY

The media often plays an important role in beginning the diffusion process by facilitating the adoption of the new behavior by a small minority of people. Research suggests, however, that once a minority of people have adopted a new sustainable behavior that personal conversations play the pivotal role in the behavior being adopted more broadly.[13]

Commitments can be combined with social diffusion to influence the rapid adoption of a new behavior. In an important study, residents who had been previously identified as putting their grass clippings

CASE STUDY

Protecting Watersheds

The Redwood River Clean Water Project is a wonderful example of social diffusion in action.[15] This program's goals were to reduce sediment and nutrients in the watershed, increase game fish habitat, fishing, reduce peak flows, and increase watershed awareness. While this project targeted watershed protection, aspects of the initiative can be applied to other sustainable behavioral change programs.

The Redwood River watershed covers an area of 703 square miles. Rather than deliver programs that encompassed the whole watershed, the watershed was divided into five sub-watersheds, which varied in size from 41.5 to 120 square miles, and the Redwood River corridor, which is 295 square miles in size. This division allowed the behavior change to be tackled at a scale that would encourage community involvement.

Farmers were encouraged to engage in best management practices (BMPs) through one-on-one conversations. These BMPs included, among others, grassed waterways, conservation tillage, riparian buffer strips, and nutrient management. These practices limit

© Guy J. Sagi, Shutterstock

at the curbside for disposal, were assigned into two groups.[14] The first group was approached and asked to make a commitment to leave their clippings on their lawn. The second was asked to make a commitment to grass cycle and to ask their neighbors to do the same. The "commitment only" request had no effect on grass cycling. However, those who were asked to speak to their neighbors, as well as make a personal commitment to grass cycle, increased not only their own grass cycling, but also that of their neighbors. Importantly, these findings were still observable 12 months later.

soil erosion and pollution run-off. Design and financial assistance was available to assist with the implementation of these BMPs.

Farmers were engaged via personal one-on-one visits, but also by hearing of BMPs that were utilized by other farmers. This information was disseminated through newsletters, handouts, and public meetings and events. Social diffusion was facilitated through the one-on-one meetings, the dissemination of information about the program, but also through a uniquely designed booklet.

The booklet included a map of the sub-watersheds along with information on BMPs and what actions farmers had taken to protect the watershed. Information on the actions of farmers was accompanied by a photo of the farmer(s), description of what actions they had taken and the results, along with a map providing driving instructions to their farm! The handbook was distributed to both participating and non-participating farmers. It normalized the use of the BMPs and encouraged discussions between farmers regarding these practices. Its distribution also increased the likelihood that farmers who adopted repetitive BMPs, like nutrient management, would continue with these practices.

Over the first five years of its existence, the Redwood River Clean Water Project enlisted 159 participants who collectively engaged in 350 BMPs and other conservation practices. By its fifth year of existence, this project was resulting in soil and phosphorous reductions of over 158 tons a year.

Note that the booklet used in this project could be tailored for a wide variety of other initiatives, such as energy efficiency in office buildings or a program to increase the use of soy-based inks by printers. As indicated above, the booklet serves two important purposes. First, it assists in the diffusion of the targeted behavior. Second, it increases the probability that those that have elected to adopt these alternative practices will stay with them.

Social diffusion is hampered when the behavior to be fostered is invisible. Unlike curbside recycling, in which engagement in the behavior is visible every time someone puts their container at the curbside, composting, like many other sustainable behaviors, occurs out of view. How can composting, and other residential behaviors, be made more visible? Attaching stickers that proclaim "We Compost Too" to the side of the recycling or garbage container can help to create and maintain community visibility for this behavior.

Whenever possible, seek commitments that are both public and durable. The sticker below was used in a program to encourage backyard composting in Nova Scotia, Canada. Households were called and asked if they composted. If they did, they were asked to place the sticker on their curbside recycling container. Placing stickers, such as the one below, on a curbside container has several positive benefits. First, each time the recycling container is taken to the curb it profiles that the household is engaged in backyard composting. Due to the importance of behaving consistently, which was discussed in the chapter on commitment, the likelihood that the household will continue to engage in composting has been increased. Second, a behavior that would otherwise be invisible in the community has been made visible. By making the behavior visible, we increase the likelihood of fostering both social diffusion and descriptive social norms. Behaviors that remain invisible will diffuse slowly and are unlikely to become normative.

© Valley Region, Nova Scotia, Canada

Here are some guidelines for using these stickers:

1. **LAMINATION:** Use a heavily laminated sticker with good adhesive so that the sticker will last for several years.

2. **PERMISSION:** Ask the household for permission to place the sticker on their recycling container as compared to asking them to place the sticker on themselves. While engagement in an activity has been found to enhance commitment, asking for permission dramatically increases the number of stickers that show up in a community. In a project that I worked on in California, over 80% agreed to place stickers on their recycling containers, but only 26% did. In contrast, when permission to place stickers on containers was obtained, and households were simply asked to place their recycling containers at the curbside in a community in Massachusetts, the number of stickers that were affixed more than doubled.

3. **VISIBILITY:** Ensure that the sticker and the text on it is visible from a distance. To ensure visibility, the sticker on the opposite page was the size of a car bumper sticker.

VISIBILITY

Making a behavior visible in a community can dramatically alter how quickly it diffuses to others. Use public and durable commitments to make behaviors that would otherwise be invisible, visible.

A CHECKLIST FOR USING SOCIAL DIFFUSION

Follow these guidelines in implementing social diffusion in your programs.

✓ As just noted, ensure that the behavior you are promoting is visible.

✓ Gain commitments from early adopters to speak to others about the behavior.

✓ Carefully identify who to target. For example, geographic information systems (GIS) are now being used along with satellite imagery to determine not only vulnerable areas of a watershed, but also what actions have already been taken by landowners. Because these systems are able to detect geographic features, such as grassed waterways, they can be used to identify early adopters who might be targeted as part of a campaign to foster social diffusion. Ben Tyson and his colleagues are already supplementing GIS systems with information regarding landowners receptivity to engaging in best management practices.[16]

Below are a variety of examples of how social diffusion can be used to foster sustainable behavior.

Examples: Using Social Diffusion to Foster Sustainable Behavior

 Agriculture & Conservation

▸ Use booklets, such as the one described in the case study in this chapter, to foster the adoption of best management practices.

Energy

▸ Residential energy efficiency actions are for the most part invisible to other residents. Increase their visibility by obtaining public and durable commitments that showcase these actions. One such program in Canada involves residents having their photos taken while holding a pledge board in front of them. These photos are then displayed in public settings and on the internet.

→

Transportation

▶ Bear Creek Elementary School in Boulder, Colorado encouraged children to walk or bike to school. One component of this program includes children being given different colored arm bands based on the distance they have travelled to school via biking and walking. The arm bands generate conversations amongst the children about walking and biking to school.

Waste & Pollution

▶ Encourage the use of reusable water containers or the picking up of litter at children's recreation centers by having teams have their photos taken and placed under a display committing to bring reusable water containers and/or to pick up litter. The display serves as a reminder of their commitment, and enhances social diffusion.

Water

▶ Ask households if a sticker can be placed on their curbside recycling container showcasing that their household reduces indoor and outdoor water use.

Prompts: Remembering to Act

> *Consistency is contrary to nature,*
> *contrary to life. The only completely*
> *consistent people are the dead.*
>
> **Aldous Huxley**

Many people have bought cotton shopping bags to use in place of the plastic bags provided by stores. While we expect that the people who have bought these bags prefer to use them whenever they shop, I also expect that like myself, they frequently leave them behind in the house or car. The problem is not a lack of motivation to use the bags, but rather simply forgetting to bring them.

Numerous actions that promote sustainability are susceptible to the most human of traits: forgetting. Turning off computer equipment, turning down the thermostat in the evening, checking the air pressure in our tires and selecting products that have recycled content while shopping are just a few of the many actions that we are apt to forget to do. In some cases, innovations such as a programmable thermostat can free us from the burden of continually remembering to carry out an activity. Most repetitive actions, however, have no simple "technological fix."

Fortunately, "prompts" are effective in reminding people to engage in sustainable behaviors. A prompt is a visual or auditory aid which reminds us to carry out an activity that we might otherwise forget. The purpose of a prompt is not to change attitudes or increase motivation, but simply to remind us to engage in an action that we are already predisposed to do.

PROMPTS AND SUSTAINABLE BEHAVIOR

Prompts abound. Slogans, such as "Think Globally, Act Locally," are, as Gardner and Stern suggest, designed to promote sustainable behaviors.[1] Despite a prevalent belief that prompts such as this are effective in promoting sustainable behavior, non-explicit prompts ordinarily have little or no impact. Prompts that target specific behaviors can, however, have a substantial impact. Here are several examples:

▶ In a water efficiency project in Perth, Australia the application of prompts to various household devices, such as taps, reduced water use by 23%.[2] Simply providing households with an informational pamphlet encouraging reductions in water use had no impact, however. This study underscored the importance of presenting a prompt in close proximity to the behavior to be encouraged.

▶ In a project in the Netherlands, providing a prompt over a waste receptacle that activated either personal or social norms regarding littering, resulted in a 50% reduction in litter.[3]

▶ In a study with significant implications, the presence of lids which indicated which recyclables should go in which recycling containers increased beverage recycling by 34% and significantly reduced contamination.[4]

▶ Jeffrey Smith and Russell Bennett have shown that prompts can be very effective in discouraging people from walking across lawns.[5] At four separate locations, 79% of pedestrians were found to cut across a lawn rather than taking a slightly longer pathway. However, when a sign with the message, "Do not cut across the

LEARNING MORE

To learn more about prompts, search the Fostering Sustainable Behavior website (cbsm.com) databases using "prompts" as the search term.

grass," was placed at these four sites, lawn-walking decreased by 46%. Lawn-walking was reduced even further when a second sign was added that said "Cutting across the grass will save 10 seconds." Indeed, when these two signs were present, lawn-walking was reduced to only 8%.

▶ Prompts by themselves have not been found to be effective in encouraging pet owners to pick up after their dogs. However, when signs were combined with modeling of the desired behavior, 80% of dog owners picked up after their pet.[6]

▶ Litter receptacles serve as a visual prompt for the proper disposal of garbage. Simply making a litter receptacle more visually interesting was found to double the amount of litter deposited in one study and increase it by 61% in another.[7,8]

▶ Retrofitting older buildings is the most effective way to reduce their energy use, but for many organizations the cost of a retrofit is prohibitive.[9] Simple lifestyle changes can, however, have a significant impact upon energy use, often with no capital expense. One such example involved encouraging university faculty to drop and tilt their blinds when they left their offices at the end of the day to reduce night-time heat loss during the winter. Baseline data was collected by cleaning staff who recorded whether blinds were dropped and tilted correctly (concave surface of the blind tilted into the room to deflect heat back into the room). Faculty were encouraged to drop-and-tilt their blinds through a general written request from the university president and by having the cleaning staff leave a reminder on the desk of faculty who forgot to drop-and-tilt their blinds. These two simple methods increased the percentage of faculty who adjusted their blinds from less than 10% to roughly two-thirds.

▶ Compared to baseline, the introduction of more conveniently located recycling containers and the use of prompts increased the amount of newspaper recycled in three apartment complexes from 50% to 100%.[10]

▶ Following the introduction of verbal and visual prompts in a high school cafateria, littering was reduced by over 350%.[11]

▶ Prompts have also been shown to have a substantial impact upon paper recycling.[12] In one department at Florida State University, a prompt that read "Recyclable Materials" was placed directly above a recycling container. The prompt indicated the types of paper to be recycled, while another prompt over the trash receptacle read "No Paper Products." The addition of these two simple prompts increased the percentage of fine paper captured by 54%, while in another department the same procedure increased the capture rate by 29%.

PROXIMITY

To be effective, prompts need to presented in close proximity to the behavior they are meant to promote.

These and other studies support the notion that to be effective, a prompt should be delivered as close in space and time as possible to the target behavior. Accordingly, place prompts to turn off lights on or beside the light switch by the exit. Similarly, prompts to purchase products that contain recycled content should be on the store shelf directly in front of the product.

PROMPTS AND SOURCE REDUCTION

Several initiatives to encourage source reduction are demonstrating just how effective prompts can be in promoting sustainable behavior.

The Minnesota Office of Waste Management has designed a program entitled SMART (Saving Money And Reducing Trash) that provides communities with various educational materials for shoppers. One element of this program is the "shelf talker." Shelf talkers are prompts that identify products that reduce waste and save money. Similarly, the Central States Education Center in Champaign, Illinois uses posters, flyers and shelf labels to indicate products that are environmentally friendly.[13] This program identifies items that either are recyclable locally, have less packaging, or are "safer-earth" products (e.g., non-toxic cleaners). Affixing 700 long-term labels throughout a store takes several hours, considerably less time than it takes to adjust the 17,000 price labels that, on average, are changed weekly. Analysis of supermarket store inventory suggests that the use of these prompts has shifted purchases to recyclable containers.

The impact upon the purchase of "least-waste packages" and "safer earth products" has not yet been determined.[14]

In Seattle, Washington, a "Get in the Loop, Buy Recycled" campaign has been operating for several years.[15] Like the other initiatives, this program utilized shelf talkers that identify products with recycled content. The program was advertised through television, radio and newspaper advertisements by both the King County Commission for Marketing Recyclable Materials and participating retailers. In the year that it was initially launched, 850 retailers in western Washington state participated. Relative to the month preceding the initial launch of the campaign, sales of recycled-content products increased nearly 30%.[16] Sales of specific product categories have shown even more dramatic increases. For example, sales of recycled-content paper products have increased by 74%.

BUILDING PROMPTS INTO YOUR PROGRAM

Prompts can be effective for encouraging both one-time and repetitive behaviors that promote sustainability. One-time behaviors, as the name suggests, refer to actions that individuals engage in only once, but that result in an ongoing positive environmental impact (e.g., installing a clock thermostat, connecting a low-flow shower head). Because these behaviors only have to be engaged in once, they are often easier to influence than repetitive behaviors, where an individual has to engage in an action repeatedly for there to be a significant environmental benefit (e.g., composting, source reduction). Given the difficulty of making lifestyle changes that promote sustainability, prompts may be of particular use in establishing and maintaining repetitive behaviors that favor sustainability.

A CHECKLIST FOR USING PROMPTS

In considering using prompts, follow these guidelines.

✓ Make the prompt noticeable.

✓ The prompt should be self-explanatory. Through graphics and/or text the prompt should explain simply what the person is to do (e.g., turn off the lights).

Reducing Outdoor Water Use

In an intriguing test of the efficacy of community-based social marketing relative to traditional information-intensive methods, three Canadian regions each delivered outdoor water efficiency programs to 500 homes in their region.[17] These homes were similar in property size, demographics and age of the home. Measurement of reductions in water use in all three regions were based upon a meter that was installed on the water mains that serviced the three groups of homes.

The region that used the traditional information-intensive approach delivered a water efficiency brochure and rain gauge to their 500 residents. Later, they provided these same residents with a reminder tag that could be placed over their outdoor water faucet. This program resulted in a 1% reduction in water use and cost $22 Canadian per household to deliver.

The two other regions used a community-based social marketing approach which involved students, in one region, and staff in the other, going door-to-door and speaking to residents about the importance of reducing outdoor water use. In each case, households were asked to make a commitment to reducing outdoor water use by placing a sticker in the front window of their home.

These stickers acknowledged that the household was working to reduce outdoor water use. They were also asked if a prompt could be placed over their outdoor water faucet. One version of this prompt is pictured on the previous page. The prompt was made of plastic to withstand water damage and reminded residents to consider whether it was

© *Region of Durham*

an odd or even day (lawn watering in these regions was to occur on odd or even days based on house number and calendar date), whether it had rained in the last week, and finally, that lawns need only a small amount of water per week to remain healthy.

The visits by students cost on average $44 Canadian per household and resulted in a 32% reduction in outdoor water use. The visits by staff, in contrast, cost $18 per household and resulted in a 45% reduction in outdoor water use (staff salaries were not included in these per capita costs). It is unclear whether the difference in water reductions between these two regions is due to a potential perceived difference in the credibility of who was delivering the message (students versus staff), differences between the regions, or both. It is also worth noting that despite the success of the two community-based social marketing programs in reducing outdoor water use, both used a relatively weak form of commitment. The commitment window stickers were only viewable by someone standing on the front doorstep. A more public display of commitment could have involved placing stickers on the side of recycling containers where the household's commitment would have been more easily viewed. As noted in the chapter on commitment, the use of recycling container commitments is also likely to foster social norms and social diffusion in a neighborhood.

The return on investment of these three programs was also calculated. The information-intensive approach brought about such small changes in outdoor water use that it was found to be not cost-effective. In contrast, even though the two community-based social marketing approaches cost more to deliver, they both brought about such significant reductions in water use that both were found to be cost-effective to deliver on a larger scale.

© Region of Durham

✓The prompt should be presented as close in time and space as possible to the targeted behavior (e.g., place a prompt to turn off lights directly on a light switch; place a prompt to purchase a product with recycled content directly below the product).

✓Use prompts to encourage people to engage in positive behaviors rather than to avoid environmentally harmful actions.

Below are several examples of how prompts can be used to foster sustainable behavior.

Examples: Using Prompts to Foster Sustainable Behavior

 Agriculture & Conservation

▸ Provide farmers with calendars that prompt conservation actions. A calendar produced by Ducks Unlimited that did this significantly affected the behavior of farmers.

Energy

▸ Affix decals directly to light switches to prompt that lights be turned off when rooms are vacant. Do the same with thermostats to encourage that temperatures be turned up or down when a home will be vacant.

▸ Affix decals to dishwashers and washing machines encouraging that they only be used when there is a full load and with cold water.

▸ Affix decals to appliances which indicate the relative energy efficiency of the appliance. This is presently done for major appliances in Canada.

Transportation

▶ Use signs to encourage drivers to turn off their engines while parked in locations where drivers frequently wait, such as schools, train stations, and loading docks.

▶ Affix removable decals to the windows of new cars prompting drivers to turn off their engines while parked.

▶ Use prompts along with commitments to encourage car owners to have their car engines regularly tuned-up and their tires properly inflated.

 Waste & Pollution

▶ Use prompts at the point of sale to promote source reduction.

▶ Distribute grocery list pads that remind shoppers every time they look at their grocery list to shop for products that have recycled content, are recylable, or have least-waste packaging.

▶ Place signs at the entrances to supermarkets reminding shoppers to bring their reusable shopping bags into the store. Also, distribute car window stickers with the purchase of reusable shopping bags; the stickers can be put on the window next to the car lock to remind people to bring their reusable bags into the store.

▶ Have check-out clerks ask consumers if they have brought bags with them.

▶ Affix decals to potentially hazardous household products during home assessments that indicate vividly that the product must be disposed of properly. The decal should contain information on where to dispose of hazardous waste and a contact number.

▶ Attach a decal to the side of recycling containers indicating what can be recycled.

 Water

▶ To encourage that lawns are watered only when necessary, ask homeowners for permission to place a tag on the outside water faucet.

▶ Arrange with local retailers to attach decals to lawnmowers that encourage householders to raise the level of the lawnmower. Additionally, this decal can encourage that the grass clippings be left on the lawn (mulched) as a natural nutrient.

▶ Have homeowners place an empty tuna can in the garden (to measure adequate watering). When the can is filled with water the garden or lawn has been adequately watered.

Communication: Creating Effective Messages

> " *My opinion, my conviction, gains*
> *infinitely in strength and success, the*
> *moment a second mind has adopted it.*
>
> **Novalis**

The morning that I began to write this chapter for the first edition of this book, my then four year-old daughter and I had breakfast together. She often used breakfast as a time to plan what we would do together when I returned from work. At four, she had already mastered many of the finer points of persuasion. She understood that to persuade me she must first secure my attention. Further, she realized that she must compete with her sister, my wife, the radio, the morning newspaper and my own preoccupations, if she was going to obtain a commitment to do one of her favorite things when I returned from work.

She usually secured my attention by asking that I sit with her at the children's table in our kitchen. This table had only two chairs, was secluded in a corner and, given its small size, placed us very close together. Further, the table was too small to place the morning paper on. From her perspective, the setting was perfect.

Once I was sitting at the table and she had my full attention, the real persuasion occurred. That summer, my daughter had three activities that she preferred above all others: going for a hike at a nearby beaver pond, having a picnic and swim at the wading pool, or going to the playground down the street (which just happened to be very close to the best place to get ice cream in Fredericton).

She rarely began by suggesting all three options. Instead, she began with the most preferred and least likely, going to the beaver pond. She understood that we rarely went to the beaver pond as we had to drive some distance to get there, so on any particular day she had little chance of persuading me to take her there. Nevertheless, she always started with the beaver pond. On that particular morning, when I begin to explain why we couldn't go to the beaver pond (we were there the night before), she cut me off by saying: "I've got a deal for you. We won't go to the beaver pond, but we can go to the wading pool and have a picnic." On that particular evening, we had a friend coming for dinner and so the picnic was quickly ruled out. Finally, she strategically turned to her third option: going to the playground down the street. Unconsciously she understood that she had the upper hand as she has already conceded the beaver pond and the wading pool. As a skilled negotiator, she knew that it was my turn to make a concession. Once she realized that I was beginning to say yes, she closed the deal by suggesting that after the playground we could get some of the ice cream that I like (she made no mention of her having any). As soon as I agreed, she immediately said, "It's a deal, then?" As I acknowledged "it's a deal," she got up from the table to tell her sister that we were going to the playground after supper (making my commitment public), and then for ice cream, while I was left to ponder, how once again, I had been out maneuvered by a four-year-old.

Much of human communication involves persuasion. Whether done by a four-year-old or a marketing firm, the aims are the same: to influence our attitudes and/or our behavior. The transition to a sustainable future will require that the vast majority of people be persuaded to adopt different lifestyles. How can we most effectively persuade people to adopt lifestyles supportive of sustainability? The purpose of this chapter is to outline some of the critical aspects of effective persuasion.

USE CAPTIVATING INFORMATION

All persuasion begins with capturing attention. Without attention, persuasion is impossible. In a review of pamphlets and flyers produced by governmental agencies and utilities on energy conservation, Paul Stern and Elliot Aronson found that most of the reviewed materials did not meet this most basic requirement.[1] The material reviewed was inconspicuous, boring or both.

How do we capture the attention then of those we wish to persuade? While, ideally, we would like to sit them down at a very small corner table, where we know we have their undivided attention, we have to resort to other means. One of the most effective ways to ensure attention is to present information that is vivid, concrete and personalized.

There are a variety of ways in which information can be made vivid, concrete and personal. For example, in a home energy audit a home assessor might utilize the householder's utility bills to underscore money that is being lost by not retrofitting. Furthermore, the assessor can provide information about similar people who have installed resource-conserving devices or describe "super-conservers" who have been exceptionally effective in reducing resource consumption.[2]

The power of vividly presented information has been demonstrated in a unique experiment carried out in California.[3] Marti Hope Gonzales and her colleagues trained nine of Pacific Gas and Electric's home assessors to present information in a manner that was psychologically compelling (they were also trained to seek a commitment). Normally, assessors provide feedback to the householder regarding energy efficiency by noting the lack of insulation in a basement or attic, cracks around windows or doors, etc. However, in this study, the assessors were trained to present this same information vividly. Below is an example of what the assessors were trained to say:

> You know, if you were to add up all the cracks around and under these doors here, you'd have the equivalent of a hole the size of a football in your living room wall. Think for a moment about all the heat that would escape from a hole that size. That's why I recommend you

VIVID INFORMATION

Presenting your communications vividly increases the likelihood of capturing your audiences' attention, while also increasing the likelihood of your information being remembered at a later time.

install weather-stripping ... And your attic totally lacks insulation. We professionals call that a naked attic. It's as if your home is facing winter not just without an overcoat, but without any clothing at all. (p. 1052)

Writing on the importance of presenting information vividly in home assessments, the authors state:

Psychologically, a crack is seen as minor, but a hole the size of a football feels disastrous. The fact that they encompass the same area is of interest to an engineer; but in the mind of the average homeowner, the football will loom larger than the cracks under the door. Similarly, insulation is something with which most people lack experience, but the idea of a naked attic in the winter is something that forces attention and increases the probability of action. (p. 1052)

Similarly, in describing the amount of waste produced annually by Californians, Shawn Burn, at California Polytechnic State University, depicts the waste as "enough to fill a two-lane highway, ten feet deep from Oregon to the Mexican border."[4] Clearly, her depiction is much more vivid than simply saying that Californians each produce 1,300 lbs. of waste annually.

Why is vivid information effective? Vivid information increases the likelihood that a message will be attended to initially, a process called encoding, as well as recalled later. That is, information that is vivid is likely to stand out against all the other information that is competing for our attention. Furthermore, because it is vivid, we are more likely to remember the information at a later time. This last point is critical, since if the information is only remembered fleetingly, it is not likely to have any long-lasting impact on our attitudes or behavior.

Research into the public's understanding of resource use demonstrates that the public has a poor understanding of household energy consumption.[5,6] Householders grossly overestimate the resources used by visible devices such as lighting and greatly underestimate less visible resource consumption, such as water heaters and furnaces. Indeed, in one study homeowners were found to believe that lighting and water heaters consumed an equivalent amount of energy. This lack of understanding is reasonable, given the dearth of information that utility bills provide regarding home resource use. This void of information has been compared to going grocery shopping and discovering that none of the items that you wish to purchase have a price tag.[7] All you receive when you go through the checkout is a total for the items purchased, you are left on your own to estimate the cost of each item. To overcome this lack of information and the public's bias toward visible sources of energy use, create a graph that shows the percentage of home energy use by item. Rather than using bars for the graph, instead replace each bar with a picture of the item itself (furnace, water heater, major appliances, lighting, etc.). By presenting information in this vivid format, you enable householders to clearly see where they should be putting most of their efforts to reduce energy use.

Once you have found a way to gain the attention of your intended audience, you next need to consider who your audience is.

KNOW YOUR AUDIENCE

Before you craft the content of your message and decide when and how you will present it, you need to know the attitudes, beliefs and behavior of your intended audience. In reality, rarely do you have just one audience. The messages you develop will need to be tailored to the different segments of the community that you wish to reach. For example, a program to decrease the purchase of household hazardous waste (HHW) and increase the incidence of household hazardous waste being taken to a depot for disposal, might target several different audiences. Preliminary research would need to determine if those who purchase HHW differ based upon the type of product; for example, household cleaner versus motor oil. Furthermore, you would need to know who would be most likely to collect the HHW in the household, and who would be most likely to take it to the depot.

Clearly, what is seemingly a relatively straightforward program has the potential to have multiple audiences for whom messages will need to be developed. To develop an effective program, therefore, you need to gather as much information as possible about the target audiences to determine how best you can communicate your messages to them. Gathering this type of information is frequently done through the use of surveys and focus groups. (See the chapter on uncovering barriers and benefits for further information.)

Another reason for knowing your audience is provided by the following example. Imagine you wished to advocate that people adopt simpler, less consumptive lifestyles. You need to know both how receptive people are to such a message, as well as how many people would presently describe themselves as living such a lifestyle. A phone survey can be used to gather this information. Phone surveys and focus groups will also allow you to gauge the level of support for a variety of more and less extreme messages regarding less consumptive lifestyles. In doing this preliminary research, you are trying to find a message that has moderate support. If you have the resources to target your message to different sectors of the community, you will need to determine the level of support within each of these sectors, for example, single parents or the elderly. Why concern yourself with finding a message that has general support? Obviously, you don't want a message that is fully supported, or you will simply be communicating what people already believe. However, you do not want to present a message that is too far removed from the beliefs of your audience. If your message is perceived to be too extreme, your audience will actually become less, rather than more, supportive. In summary, then, you want to tailor your message so that it is slightly more extreme than the beliefs of your audience. Messages that are just slightly more extreme are likely to be embraced. Over time, it is possible to move people's attitudes and beliefs a great deal. However, you will need to have the patience and resources to do this as it is achieved one small step at a time.

USE A CREDIBLE SOURCE

Who presents your message can have a dramatic impact upon how it is received. In general, the more credible the person or organization delivering the message, the more influence there will be upon the audience.[8] The impact of credibility upon sustainable behavior is demonstrated in the following study. In this study, two groups of

ANALYZE BEHAVIORS

As discussed in the chapter on uncovering barriers and benefits, breaking a behavior down to the actions that comprise it is a tremendously useful tool in identifying different target audiences. Understanding the barriers that exist for different audiences will greatly enhance your ability to develop effective communications.

homes received an identical pamphlet on energy conservation. In one case, the pamphlet was enclosed in an envelope from the State Regulatory Agency, while in the other the envelope was from the local utility. Prior research had shown that the State Regulatory Agency was viewed as more credible than the local utility, but would simply enclosing the same pamphlet in the two different envelopes have an impact upon home energy use? The answer was, yes. Those householders who received the pamphlet from the State Regulatory Agency carried out more of the advocated changes than did the householders who received the identical pamphlet from the local utility.[9]

How do you determine who will be credible for your audience? One method is to use a survey to determine the credibility of several different spokespersons or organizations. A simpler method, however, is to search for organizations or individuals who are well known for their expertise in the area and have the public's trust. Perceived credibility appears to be based primarily on these two attributes. You might also consider having your initiative endorsed by a number of credible individuals. Endorsement from several sources is more likely to be effective, since some individuals will be more credible to some segments of the public, while other individuals will be more credible to others.

Once you have decided *who* will deliver your message, you next need to concern yourself with *what* will be communicated.

FRAME YOUR MESSAGE

Interestingly, how you present, or "frame," the activity you are trying to promote is very important. Most sustainable activities can be presented positively (You should compost because you'll save in garbage collection user fees), or negatively (If you don't compost you'll lose money by having to pay more to have your garbage collected). Understandably, most organizations gravitate toward presenting positive rather than negative motivations to engage in a new activity, but should they? Apparently, they shouldn't. Messages which emphasize losses which occur as a result of inaction are often more persuasive than messages that emphasize savings as a result of taking action.[10]

CONSIDER THE USE OF THREATENING MESSAGES CAREFULLY

Few public issues lend themselves better to threatening messages than sustainability. Evidence of the predicament we are in abounds. Issues such as species loss, climate change, ozone depletion, and air and water pollution are just a few of the many assaults on the environment and consequently ourselves. However, is it wise to use threatening messages in communicating with the public? There is no simple answer to this question, but here are some of the issues you should consider. First, literature in the field of stress and coping suggests that we need to begin by appraising an issue as a threat before we are likely to take appropriate action.[11] Rachel Carson's ground-breaking book, *Silent Spring*, for example, demonstrated the importance and effectiveness of communicating imminent threats to a wide audience. However, to be effective, threatening messages need to communicate more than just the threat we face. In response to a threat, people have what Richard Lazarus refers to as two broad coping strategies. Lazarus' research suggests that individuals respond to threats by using either problem-focused coping, or emotion-focused coping. Problem-focused coping, as the name suggests, refers to taking direct action to alleviate the threat. In the case of global warming, problem-focused coping might entail using alternative transportation, or increasing the energy efficiency of your home. In contrast, emotion-focused coping might involve ignoring the issue, changing the topic whenever it is raised in conversation, or denying that there is anything that can or needs to be done. Whether someone uses problem-focused coping or emotion-focused coping appears to be determined by their perception of how much control they have to correct the problem. If we perceive that we have a significant amount of control, we are likely to use problem-focused coping. If we perceive that we have very little, we are likely to use emotion-focused coping. Further, research that I have conducted suggests that our perception of how much control we have regarding global issues is largely determined by our sense of community.[12] If we feel that, in concert with others, we can have an impact, we are likely to act. If, however, we feel little common purpose, we are likely to perceive that there is little we can do personally.

Threatening or fear-arousing messages need to be combined with clear suggestions regarding what people can do to reduce the threat. Using threatening messages, then, needs to be carefully considered. It is important that your audience understands the gravity of the situation. However, if you are not able to engender a feeling of common purpose and efficacy in dealing with the threat at the same time, your message may cause people to avoid, rather than constructively deal with the issue.

In summary, threatening messages are a necessary part of directing people's attention to crises. However, they are likely to be counter-productive if they are not coupled with messages that are empowering. Furthermore, repeatedly presenting a threatening message can cause people to habituate to the message. Once people understand the "crisis," it is wise to move primarily to dealing with solutions.

DECIDE ON A ONE-SIDED VERSUS TWO-SIDED MESSAGE

All issues have more than one side. However, in developing persuasive communication, should you address just one or both sides? The answer, as with most things in life, is "it depends." If you are presenting your communication to an audience that has little comprehension of the issue, you will be most persuasive if you present just one side. However, if you are communicating with an audience that is aware of both sides of the issue, then you need to present both sides in order to be perceived as credible. As with the content of the message, deciding on a one-sided versus two-sided message underscores the importance of knowing your audience.

Presenting two sides of the issue has an additional advantage. By presenting the opposing viewpoint, and providing the counter-arguments to this viewpoint, it is possible to "inoculate" your audience against alternative views.

MAKE YOUR MESSAGE SPECIFIC

When crafting your message, you will want to ensure that the actions you advocate are clearly articulated. Messages that describe actions to be taken in clear, straightforward steps are more likely to be understood and followed. For example, rather than simply suggesting that households weather-strip, you need to show each of the steps that are involved in weather-stripping a door or window.

FEARFUL MESSAGES

Threatening messages need to be coupled with concrete and empowering information on what can be done to address a threat, such as climate change. Failing to couple threatening information with empowering suggestions may well lead your target audience to avoid an issue as they feel helpless to address it.

MAKE YOUR MESSAGE EASY TO REMEMBER

All actions that support sustainability rely upon memory. Some activities, such as recycling, make substantial demands on memory. In asking someone to recycle, we are requiring them to remember how to recycle, for example, whether it is necessary to separate or wash items, when to recycle, and what to recycle. Research suggests that failing to address the role that memory plays can significantly harm the success of a program.[13] Stuart Oskamp has demonstrated, for example, that recycling programs which make it easy to remember how to recycle, by having the recyclable items commingled rather than separated, have higher participation and substantially higher capture rates. Of course, this effect might also be due to greater convenience.[14] Furthermore, programs that make it easy to remember when to recycle by having recycling occur on the same day as garbage collection, also report higher participation rates.[15] Finally, the public can find it quite difficult to remember what to recycle. Many curbside recycling programs have extensive lists of recyclable items. Indeed, when the I once asked the project team who had developed the promotional and educational recycling materials for a large municipality to name all of the items that could be recycled, none could. Research suggests that the public knows the main items that can be recycled, such as glass, cans, and newspaper, but has a great deal of difficulty in remembering many other items. In contrast, remembering what to compost is significantly easier. People can create a simple memory device, or heuristic, to guide them in remembering what to compost. For example, if it is food waste or yard waste it is compostable, as long as it is not meat, oil or dairy. In contrast, no simple memory device will work for recycling since there is no unifying theme that unites all the items.

One of the simplest ways to remove the burden that a sustainable activity can place upon memory is through the use of prompts. Remember that, to be effective, the prompt needs to be presented as close as possible to where the activity is going to occur. See the chapter on prompts for further information. Affixing a prompt to the side of a recycling container meets this criterion of proximity and may be more useful than providing prompts that are affixed to a fridge. It may, in fact, be advantageous to provide both since some households do not collect recyclables in their recycling container. Similarly, attaching a prompt to a kitchen-organics catcher can make it easy for people to remember what can be composted, and cut down on contamination rates.

Remember, unless we make it easy for people to remember how, when, and what to do, it is unlikely that a program will be very successful.

PROVIDE PERSONAL OR COMMUNITY GOALS

Providing targets for a household or a community to reach can be effective in reducing energy and water use and in increasing waste reduction. A national survey of the directors of 264 U.S. recycling programs revealed that those cities that had set community recycling goals were more successful than those that had not. Clearly, these programs likely differed in other important ways as well.[16]

This recycling container sticker by Sonoma County, California makes it significantly easier to remember what to recycle by grouping items (e.g., Cans & foil, Paper, etc.) and using pictures to depict the items that are recyclable. Note that using the pictures can also assist in addressing literacy issues. © Sonoma County.

EMPHASIZE PERSONAL CONTACT

Research on persuasion demonstrates that the major influence upon our attitudes and behavior is not the media, but rather our contact with other people. That is not to say that the media is without influence. Advertising can be effective in two ways. First, it is effective when the objective is to increase market share by switching the public from one brand of a product to another.[17] Increasing market share is a relatively easy process given that the consumer is already committed to purchasing a type of product and there are few impediments to altering brand loyalties. Second, the media has an indirect effect by influencing the topics that we discuss. For example, the media may not directly influence you to be more energy efficient, but if you watch a documentary on climate change, and subsequently discuss it, the conversation you have may convince you to make your home more efficient.

MODEL SUSTAINABLE BEHAVIOR

Whether the contact is made personally or through the media, one of the more effective methods for increasing adoption of a sustainable behavior is to model the behavior we wish others to adopt. Modeling involves demonstrating a desired behavior.[18] Modeling can occur in person, or through television or internet-based instructional videos. For example, studies have documented significant reductions in energy use in response to a broadcast that demonstrated simple energy efficient actions and mentioned the financial benefits to be gained from carrying them out.[19,20]

COMMUNITY BLOCK LEADERS

Commitment, modeling, norms and social diffusion all have at their core, the interaction of individuals in a community. Commitment occurs when one individual pledges to another to carry out some form of activity. Modeling results when we observe the actions of others. Norms develop as people interact and develop guidelines for their behavior, and social diffusion occurs as people pass information to one another regarding their experiences with new activities. Research has documented that it is possible to harness these processes in order to have a significant impact on the adoption of sustainable behaviors. By making use of community volunteers or block leaders, Shawn Burn has demonstrated the powerful and cost-effective impact that some of these factors can have.[21] Working with city officials in Claremont, California, she arranged to have homes that were not recycling randomly divided into three groups: the first received a persuasive appeal delivered by a block leader; the second received a written persuasive appeal; and the third was a control group. Both the persuasive appeal delivered by the block leader and the written persuasive appeal made use of the same message. Homes in the control group were not approached and served as a comparison for the other conditions. In the condition in which a persuasive appeal was delivered by a block leader, homeowners were approached by individuals from their community who were already recycling. These "block leaders" delivered a persuasive appeal and left orange recycling bags with the homeowner. In the persuasive message-alone condition, homeowners received a written version of the same message and the recycling bags. In the 10 weeks that followed the delivery of the messages, the results firmly supported the block leader approach as being most effective. An average of 28% of the homes visited by the block leader recycled weekly, compared with 12% for those who received only the written appeal, and only 3% for the control group. Further, over 58% of those households in the "block leader" condition recycled at least once in the follow-up, compared with 38% for the written appeal and 19.6% for the control group. It should be note that the use of block leaders need not be limited to recycling. It could have been used similarly to promote a variety of activities such as composting, source reduction, energy conservation or water efficiency.

LEVERAGE CONTACT

As discussed in the chapter on commitments, leverage brief personal contacts, such as by phone, to obtain commitments to review printed materials that are subsequently dropped off a home or business. The brief personal contact can substantially increase the likelihood of your printed materials be attended to.

PROVIDE FEEDBACK

Effective communications involve more than simply presenting information to persuade people to adopt a new activity, or making it easy for them to remember what, when and how to do the activity. To be fully effective, information about the impact of newly adopted activities needs to be presented as well. Numerous studies document the impact that providing feedback can have upon the adoption and maintenance of sustainable behavior. Here are several examples:

▶ Posting signs above aluminum can recycling containers that provided feedback about the number of cans that had been recycled during the previous weeks increased capture rates by 65%.[22]

▶ Households were mailed monthly letters that indicated the extent to which they had been able to reduce energy use over the same month during the previous year. In a letter that was sent separately from their bill, they were provided both with the reduction in kWhs and cost. This simple procedure reduced energy use by nearly

CASE STUDY

Using Email to Change Behavior

Nancy Artz and Peter Cooke have utilized the Maine Department of Environmental Protection's (DEP) email system to foster the adoption of sustainable behaviors by DEP staff.[23] Emails were sent to 420 employees encouraging their engagement in four household behaviors: 1) checking tire pressure; 2) installing compact fluorescent light bulbs (CFLs); 3) checking the efficiency of their refrigerator; and 4) purchasing green power.

For each of these four behaviors, a series of emails was sent. The first email requested that the employees make a commitment to carry out a specific action. The second email was sent only to those employees who made a commitment to engage in the action and asked if they had undertaken the action. The third email was sent to all DEP employees and showcased the number of staff who had committed to engaging in the

behavior. This email served both as a way of making their commitments public as well as a way of developing descriptive norms. (See the chapters on commitments and norms

© Lasse Kristensen, Shutterstock

5% compared to similar periods during the previous two years. Furthermore, this study included a control group of households that never received this feedback. During the period of time in which the households who were receiving feedback were reducing energy use, the control households increased energy use.

▶ Households that received daily feedback on electricity consumption lowered energy use by 11%, compared to physically identical households that did not receive feedback.[24]

---

for further information.) In the case of tire inflation, for example, the first email informed DEP staff of the benefits of properly inflated tires (i.e., reduced emissions, enhanced fuel efficiency, and extended tire life). It then asked, "Will you commit to checking your tire pressure by the end of the weekend?" Recipients could respond by using Microsoft Outlook's designated reply buttons. In the case of tire inflation, the following predesignated replies were provided: 1) I already checked it within the last two weeks; 2) I will commit to checking it by the end of the weekend, thanks; 3) I'm not interested, but good luck to everyone else; and 4) Oh ... tire pressure needs to be checked?

A week later those who had made a commitment to check their tires were sent a follow-up email in which they were asked to indicate if they had checked their tires. Finally, five days later a message was sent out to all employees noting that many people had committed to checking their tires and

that the number of people who acted on that commitment was "pretty good."

How effective was this campaign? The percentage of DEP employees who responded to the initial email announcing each behavior was as follows: 41% for tires; 34% for CFLs; 32% for fridges; and 18% for green power. Of the individuals who responded, commitments to engage in the behaviors were as follows: 59% for tires, 38% for CFLs, 63% for fridges, and 8% for green power. Definitive information on what people actually did is challenging in a project such as this. However, in the case of the CFLs, the number of bulbs reported to have been installed (38) was substantially lower than the actual number of bulbs that had been purchased at the front kiosk where they had been made available for sale. The authors note that purchases at the kiosk would not reflect purchases at hardware stores. It appears what while not all employees responded to the email campaign, many were influenced by it.

▸ Households that received weekly group feedback on the total pounds of paper they had recycled increased the amount recycled by 26%.[25] When weekly feedback was combined with public commitments, there was a 40% increase.

▸ When residents of the Midland-Odessa (Texas) area were provided with conservation tips and daily feedback via television, gasoline usage was reduced by 32%.[26] Furthermore, three months after ending the feedback, gasoline usage was 15% lower than it had been prior to the program.

CHECK LIST FOR EFFECTIVE COMMUNICATIONS

This chapter has provided a variety of methods by which you can enhance the effectiveness of the communications you produce. In creating future communications, use this checklist as a guide;

✓ Make sure that your message is vivid, personal and concrete.

✓ Using the techniques described in the chapter on uncovering barriers and benefits, explore the attitudes and behavior of your intended audience prior to developing your message.

✓ Have your message delivered by an individual (or organization) who has credibility with the audience you are trying to reach.

✓ Frame your message to indicate what the individual is losing by not acting, rather than what he/she is saving by acting.

✓ If you use a threatening message, make sure that you couple it with specific suggestions regarding what actions an individual can take to remedy the situation.

✓ Use a one-sided or two-sided message depending upon the knowledge of your audience regarding the particular issue.

✓ Make your communication, especially instructions for a desired behavior, clear and specific.

LEARNING MORE

To learn more about effective communication, search the Fostering Sustainable Behavior website (cbsm.com) databases using the particular aspect of effective communication that you are interested in as the search term, such as "feedback" or "framing."

✓ Make it easy for people to remember what to do, and how and when to do it.

✓ Integrate personal or community goals into the delivery of your program.

✓ Enhance knowledge by modeling behaviors.

✓ Make sure that your program enhances social diffusion by increasing the likelihood that people will discuss their new activity with others.

✓ Where possible, use personal contact to deliver your message.

✓ Provide feedback at both the individual and community levels about the impact of sustainable behaviors.

Below are a variety of suggestions for using effective communication to promote sustainable behavior.

Examples: Using Effective Communication to Foster Sustainable Behavior

 Agriculture & Conservation

▸ Recruit individuals and/or organizations that are credible to speak to the importance of engaging in actions that enhance biodiversity.

Energy

▸ Use brightly colored door-hangers rather than flyers or bill inserts to provide feedback on energy use. Flyers and bill inserts are frequently ignored. Door hangers that are well-designed have a higher likelihood of being noticed.

▶ Provide company-wide feedback on reductions in energy use as result of personal actions, such as turning off office equipment.

 Transportation

▶ Enhance the likelihood of staff discussing alternative transportation by showcasing those who carpool, use mass transit, bike or walk to work.

 Waste & Pollution

▶ To portray vividly the amount of waste generated by a community, consider comparing it to a well-known local landmark.

▶ Life magazine once portrayed our consumptive lifestyles by taking all the possessions of an American family and placing them on the front lawn of their house. Next to this picture was a picture of a family from a developing country, once again, with all of their possessions placed in front of their home. The contrast in lifestyles and the attendant impact upon the environment were blatant. Prepare a similar display for your community.

 Water

▶ To bring attention to the amount of water that is used for lawn watering, prepare a chart that depicts the amount of water consumed for lawn watering, showering, cooking, etc. Lawn watering will dwarf the other items.

▶ Follow Canberra, Australia's lead by providing community feedback on daily water consumption via roadside digital signs.

Incentives: Enhancing Motivation to Act

> " *It is the function of vice to keep virture within reasonable bound.*
>
> **Samuel Butler**

Financial incentives can provide the motivation for individuals to perform an activity that they already engage in more effectively, such as recycling, or to begin an activity that they otherwise would not perform, such as carpooling. This chapter will provide evidence of the impact of incentives on a diverse array of sustainable behaviors and provide some general suggestions on their use.

While incentives have been used to foster a variety of sustainable behaviors, they have been applied most extensively to waste reduction. For example, a growing number of North American cities have implemented user-fee systems for garbage disposal. While significant differences exist in the methods used, reviews of user fee systems clearly indicate that they dramatically reduce the amount of waste going to landfill, and provide additional motivation for households to recycle, compost and, perhaps, source reduce.

Here are several examples:

▸ When San Jose, California introduced a user-pay program in which residents were charged based upon the size of the container they placed at the curb, the impact was a 46% decrease in waste sent to the landfill, a 158% increase in recyclables captured, and a 38% increase in yard waste collected. There was no charge for curbside recycling and yard waste collection.[1]

▸ When the Capital Regional District in British Columbia began to charge households for placing more than one bag or container at the curb there was a 21% reduction in waste going to the landfill and a 527% increase in recycling capture rates. Curbside recycling was a free service to residents and yard waste had to be taken to a depot.[2]

▸ Worchester, Massachusets introduced a program in which residents purchased bags for their garbage. This program resulted in a 45% reduction in the waste stream, with recycling responsible for 37% of the waste stream diversion. Residents were not charged for recycling nor for dropping off yard waste at a collection center.[3]

Another form of incentive is bottle deposits, where consumers pay an additional charge for purchasing beverages and then receive a portion of the deposit back when they return the container. Several studies indicate that deposits on beverage containers have a substantial impact on reducing littering:

▸ The introduction of bottle deposits has been associated with a 68% reduction in litter in Oregon, a 76% reduction in Vermont, and an 82% reduction in Michigan.[4]

▸ When beverage container deposits were introduced in New York State, analysis of a highway exit and a section of a railway track in New York revealed that there was a 74% reduction in litter of stamped 5-cent deposit returnable bottles and cans along the highway exit, and a 99% reduction along the railway track.[5]

INCENTIVES AND OTHER SUSTAINABLE BEHAVIORS

While incentives have had a remarkable impact upon waste reduction, their use in promoting other sustainable behaviors has not been as extensive. Below are a variety of examples of their use:

► Assuming that moving provided an opportunity to alter transportation choices, households that had moved recently were provided with a one-day free ride mass-transit ticket and personalized information regarding transit schedules. Comparing

---

CASE STUDY

Promoting Waste Reduction

The impact that introducing a user-fee program for garbage collection has upon waste reduction has been carefully studied in Sydney Township, Ontario. Sydney Township introduced a user-pay system in which residents received 52 free tags to place on garbage bags, with extra tags costing $1.50 Canadian each.

Sydney Township carefully monitored the impact that introducing this initiative had upon their waste stream. Relative to the previous year, garbage sent to the landfill was reduced by 46%, weight of recyclables increased by 26%, and the amount of kitchen waste being backyard composted rose to 50%. The introduction of user fees for garbage collection also decreased the amount of HHW placed in garbage by 50%.[6]

©Glue Stock, Shutterstock

transportation choices before the move and afterward, use of public transport increased from 18% of trips to 36% of trips and car use simultaneously declined, from 53% beforehand to 39% after the move.[7]

▶ The state of California provides an incentive of $.16 a gallon for do-it-yourselfers (DIYS) to return used oil to certified used oil collection centers (CCCS). In a review of the state's environmental policies regarding used oil, anecdotal evidence suggests that those returning the used oil rarely asked for payment, and the CCCS rarely offered it, limiting the impact that this incentive could have upon behavior. Interestingly, the authors suggest that since these centers are paid an equivalent amount to collect used oil to what they are to pay out for its return, they are only able to profit from its collection if they do not inform those returning the oil of the incentive's existence.[8]

LEARNING MORE

To learn more about incentives, search the Fostering Sustainable Behavior website (cbsm.com) databases using "incentives" as the search term.

▶ Unless specifically linked, there is a perceived inherent conflict between the financial performance of a company and its environmental performance. What occurs, however, if compensation for top management is linked to environmental performance of their company? In a review of the performance of various companies, only when there was explicit link between environmental performance and management compensation was there evidence of an increase in environmental performance. However, these effects were found to be limited in scope.[9]

▶ The province of Ontario, Canada initiated an aggressive program to encourage the installation of solar photovoltaic systems. Under the Renewable Energy Standard Offer program, owners of systems under 10MW can sell power to the grid at the rate of $0.42 per kWh. To encourage investment in solar power, this rate is locked in for twenty years. While this is a sizable incentive, barriers to the implementation of solar photovoltaic systems have been found to limit uptake.[10]

▶ In a review of residential energy conservation programs, rewarding the adoption of energy conservation behaviors was effective, but the impact was usually short-lived.[11]

▶ A national study of the influence of eight major conservation incentive programs in the United States found that they had a substantial impact upon forest and habitat protection.[12] Not surprisingly, landowners who have positive attitudes toward land management have been found to be most receptive to these programs.[13]

▶ Households in the United Kingdom who are on a fixed tariff system, where they pay a flat rate independent of the amount of water they use, were found, not surprisingly, to use more water than those on a variable tariff in which charges were based on actual use.[14]

▶ Cycling levels in the Netherlands, Denmark and Germany are substantially higher than those in the United Kingdom and the United States, where roughly only 1% of trips are made by bike. High levels of cycling in these three countries have been found to be related to the introduction of safe cycling laneways, traffic calming in residential areas, sufficient bike parking, and incorporation of cycling with public transport. However, cycling has also been spurred by making driving expensive through taxes on vehicle ownership, charging for driving (e.g., congestion charges), and increased parking rates.[15]

CREATING EFFECTIVE INCENTIVES

Incentives can be an important component of a community-based social marketing strategy, particularly when motivation to engage in a behavior is low. The following guidelines are drawn from Gardner and Stern's discussion of the use of incentives to foster sustainable behavior.[16]

1. **CONSIDER THE SIZE OF THE INCENTIVE.** Incentives need to be large enough to be taken seriously. However, past a certain point, diminishing returns occur from increasing the size of the

Incentive. Study the impact that incentives of different sizes have had in other communities in arriving at the size of incentive for your program.

2. **CLOSELY PAIR THE INCENTIVE AND THE BEHAVIOR.** Incentives are usually most effective when they are presented at the time the behavior is to occur. For example, charging for the use of plastic shopping bags at the checkout brings attention to the cost of using disposable bags and increases motivation to bring reusable bags. For example, at the supermarket at which I shop, the introduction of a 5-cent charge per plastic bag has resulted in approximately 60% of shoppers using reusable bags or containers for their groceries.

3. **MAKE THE INCENTIVE VISIBLE.** When implementing an incentive carefully consider how you can draw attention to it. Remember that an incentive will have little or no impact if people are unaware of its existence.

4. **USE INCENTIVES TO REWARD POSITIVE BEHAVIOR.** Research in behavior modification underscores the importance of using incentives to reward behavior we would like people to engage in. When sustainable behaviors, such as recycling, are rewarded with lower garbage disposal costs, the likelihood that people will recycle in the future increases. In contrast, disincentives are often less predictable, since the punishment suppresses an unwanted behavior but does not directly encourage a positive alternative. A concrete example of the relative effectiveness of incentives versus disincentives is provided by research in littering, which has shown that bottle deposits that reward people for not littering are far more effective than fines that punish people for littering.

5. **BE CAUTIOUS ABOUT REMOVING INCENTIVES.** The following story illustrates the importance of keeping incentives in place once they have been introduced.

A grocer was having difficulty with a group of teenage boys who visited his store each day after school.[17] Shortly after the boys arrived, they would stand outside and verbally abuse the store owner and those who shopped at the store. Indeed, their behavior was so upsetting to some customers that they began to shop elsewhere. Realizing that his business was in jeopardy, the store owner came up with an ingenious plan. The next time the boys arrived, he waited for a few minutes after they began their verbal assault. He then said something that the boys, undoubtedly, thought was remarkable. Rather than criticizing them for their behavior, instead he applauded it. He told the boys that in fact they were so good at yelling obscenities at himself and his customers, he was going to give each of them five dollars. The boys, who likely were beginning to question the sanity of the shop owner, took the money and left shortly thereafter. When they returned the following day, the owner waited once again until they had hurled insults for a few minutes and then went out and congratulated them on their efforts. He added, however, that the store had not done quite as well as it had yesterday and that all he could afford to give each of them was a dollar. The boys grumbled a little bit, but nonetheless took the money. When they returned the following day, the same events took place, but with the man explaining that he could only afford to give them a quarter each. They grumbled even more, but once again took the money. On the fourth day, he let the boys yell and shout for quite some time before he went out. When he did, he explained that the store had done particularly poorly that day and that he could not afford to pay them anything. Without hesitation the teenagers replied that there was absolutely no way that they were going to yell obscenties each day after school if they were not going to get paid, and left.

This story illustrates the danger of introducing incentives to foster a sustainable behavior and then removing them. Many individuals engage in sustainable activities, such as recycling, because it makes them feel that they are making a positive contribution. Similarly, the teenage boys originally showed up at the grocer's store each day after school because they enjoyed being obnoxious. When intrinsic motivations are replaced with incentives, or external motivations, internal motivations can be undermined. Just as the boys' intrinsic motivations were jeopardized by the store owner paying them, so can the motivation to recycle be undermined if an incentive is introduced and then removed. In short, think carefully about introducing an incentive, such as user fees, if you believe that the incentive may be removed at some later time.

AVOIDANCE

When incentives are perceived to be substantial, such as with carpooling lanes or user fees for garbage collection, people are motivated to avoid the incentive. Prior to delivering your program, review how others have dealt with this problem and plan accordingly.

6. **PREPARE FOR PEOPLE'S ATTEMPTS TO AVOID THE INCENTIVE.** When preparing to use incentives keep in mind that people can be very creative in attempting to avoid them. In Victoria, British Columbia, for example, when user fees were introduced for residential garbage collection, some residents would carry their trash downtown and dump it in one of the city street waste baskets. The City of Victoria dealt with this problem by taking out classified ads in the newspaper naming these people and them to come down to City Hall to pick up their illegally dumped trash (illegal dumpers frequently left identifying information in their garbage). After running the classified ads for a short time, the practice of "carrying garbage to work" largely stopped.

On the next page are a variety of examples of how incentives can be used to foster sustainable behavior.

Examples: Using Incentives to Foster Sustainable Behavior

 Agriculture & Conservation

▶ Provide incentives to rural landowners to create wildlife corridors.

 Energy

▶ Introduce electricity rates that increase with use.

▶ It is expensive for homeowners to upgrade insulation or install energy-efficient windows or heating/cooling systems. However, allowing for renovations to be paid through savings in energy use can make home energy retrofits far more appealing.

▶ Charge variable rates based upon time of electricity use.

▶ Provide loans, grants or rebates for home energy retrofits.

Transportation

▶ Provide incentives for multiple-occupant cars and mass transit by providing exclusive lanes that allow for faster travel times compared to single-occupant cars.

▶ Provide preferential parking for multiple-occupant cars.

Waste & Pollution

▶ Place an additional charge on beverage containers that is
  partially refunded when the container is returned.

▶ Charge for the use of items such as plastic shopping bags and
  sytrofoam cups.

▶ Use user fees to increase motivation to recycle, compost and
  source reduce.

▶ Attach a sizable deposit on HHW to provide the motivation
  necessary for individuals to take leftover products to a depot for
  proper disposal.

 Water

▶ For many homes it is too expensive to install a low-flow toilet.
  Allowing the cost of the toilet and installation to be paid for
  through savings in the water bill removes this barrier.

Convenience:
Making it Easy to Act

<blockquote>

" *All things are difficult before*
they are easy.

Thomas Fuller
</blockquote>

The previous six chapters identified a variety of tools to overcome barriers to a sustainable behavior that reside within an individual. As powerful as these tools are, they will be ineffective if the behavior is inconvenient. If the behavior is unpleasant or time-consuming, for example, no matter how well you address internal barriers your community-based social marketing strategy will be unsuccessful.

The first step to removing external barriers is to identify them. Using the techniques outlined in the chapter on barriers and benefits, attempt to isolate what external barriers exist and what can be done to address them. The City of Boulder, Colorado, for example, identified that two significant barriers to mass transit usage were workers' concerns regarding how they would get home quickly in an emergency (e.g., a sick child that has to come home from school) and, for women, safety concerns about taking mass transit late at night. These two barriers were addressed by providing a free taxi service in either of these instances.

INCONVENIENCE

Behaviors that are inconvenient have low participation levels. Failure to address this barrier assures low adoption levels.

The role of inconvenience is also evident with backyard composting. At present, approximately 30% of homeowners in the Province of Ontario participate in composting, compared with over 80% participation in curbside recycling. While many factors might explain these substantially different participation rates, it is likely that the inconvenience of obtaining a composter, and the perceived inconvenience of composting, are significant barriers. Indeed, in two studies that I conducted in different Canadian cities, inconvenience was on both occasions one of the most significant barriers to composting.[1] Furthermore, in comparing households who compost seasonally with those who compost throughout the year, the only

CASE STUDY

Making Biking Convenient

Bike-sharing programs were first launched in Amsterdam in 1965. This first foray into communal bike-sharing did not fare well, as the bikes were quickly stolen or vandalized. Thirty-five years later, however, bike-sharing programs are being implemented in cities around the world. The current generation of bikes are both durable and traceable, significantly reducing the problems that plagued early bike-sharing initiatives. As of 2009, 100 bike-sharing programs were in existence, with another 45 being introduced in 2010 alone.[5] In total, some 139,000 bikes are being shared in different programs across the globe, with some sites, such as Velib in Paris, averaging an astounding 75,000 rentals a day.[6]

The concept is disarmingly simple. Bikes are provided at convenient stations, such

as the one shown below. Users register at a station or online to use the bikes. Registrations can be for as short as a day or as long as a year. Once registered, riders either enter a code or swipe a registration card to obtain a bike, which they then drop off at another station close to their destination. Bikes that are not returned within 24 hours are considered stolen and are charged to the user's credit card.

Bike-sharing programs have several target audiences, perhaps the most important of which is commuters. Even the most extensive mass-transit systems can only get commuters close to their destination. Bike sharing allows commuters to travel the *last mile* quickly and conveniently. Additional target audiences include commuters who have driven to work, but then use the bikes for short trips. Finally, factor which was found to distinguish these two groups was the perceived inconvenience of composting in the winter (remember the anecdote with which I began this book).

Communities that provide curbside organic collection effectively eliminate several of the external barriers that exist for backyard composting. First, these communities directly provide households with containers or carts, removing the cost and inconvenience of obtaining a backyard composter from a store. Second, many of these communities provide kitchen organic catchers along with the curbside container, increasing the convenience of collecting organics. Because many of these containers often include a prompt

tourists are frequent users, particularly in cities such as Paris.

Most bike-sharing programs are franchises in which a company runs the program for a municipality in return for being able to sell advertising that is placed at the stations or on the bikes themselves.[7]

The Bixi system in Montreal, which is pictured here, is intriguing. Stations are solar-powered and can be set up in just twenty minutes. Furthermore, these stations are mobile and can be moved to different locations as demand requires, providing a level of flexibility that few other transportation programs can match.

While the impact of bike-sharing programs on emissions can be difficult to ascertain, as it is uncertain that trips taken by bike are displacing vehicle trips, the distance travelled by bike is extraordinary. In Paris alone, users of the Velib system travel over 300,000 kilometers per day. Survey research suggests that bike-sharing is displacing between 8% and 16% of vehicle trips.[8,9]

© Bixi Montreal

to identify what can be composted, learning to separate organics is also simplified. Third, unlike backyard composting, the process of curbside organic collection is nearly identical to that used for curbside recycling and garbage disposal (place in a container, take the container to the curb, periodically wash container). The similarity of this new behavior (curbside organic collection) to older, well established behaviors (recycling and garbage collection), simplifies what a household needs to learn in order to participate. The impact of making composting convenient and inexpensive by providing containers and curbside collection can produce dramatic results. In an evaluation of a curbside organic pilot, in the Halifax Regional Municipality, fully 99% of households participated. Indeed, the one household who was not participating, wanted to, but had not received a cart in which to place their organics.

It is important to assess whether it is realistic to overcome the external barriers you identify. To do this, it is useful to explore the success that other programs have had in promoting the same behavior and decide whether you have the resources to mount a similar program. Promoting the use of car pooling, mass transit, bicycling and walking as alternatives to single occupant car usage, as Boulder, Colorado has done, requires significant expenditures. In cases where the financial resources do not exist to make the new behavior more convenient, such as through building bicycle paths, consider instead making the behavior you wish to discourage less convenient and more costly. Multiple possibilities exist for making an activity such as single-occupant driving less convenient and more costly.[2,3] As described in the last chapter, many communities have instituted slower laneways on highways for single-occupant cars or have introduced traffic calming by turning two-way streets into one-way streets. Corporations have discouraged single-occupant car usage by charging more for parking for single-occupant vehicles and making the parking of these cars less convenient (e.g., farther from the building).

Making the activity you wish to discourage less convenient and more expensive can increase motivation for the behavior you wish to encourage. In short, you want to design a program that enhances motivation by making the sustainable behavior more convenient

LEARNING MORE

To learn more about convenience, search the Fostering Sustainable Behavior website (cbsm. com) databases using "convenience" as the search term.

and less costly than the alternative, non-sustainable activity. As demonstrated in the previous chapter, incentives can be effectively used to enhance motivation.

Finally, it is important to note that convenience is to some extent a matter of perception. When people have experience with an activity, they often come to see that activity as being more convenient than when they first began. In one study, as individuals gained more experience with recycling bottles they found it more convenient.[4] While a behavior that is perceived very inconvenient will need other measures, those actions that are perceived to be only somewhat inconvenient may be addressed through the use of tools such as commitment and norms.

In summary, because the nature of external barriers can vary dramatically across communities, strategies for removing these barriers will have to be tailored to each situation. Begin by identifying what external barriers exist and then seek information from other communities on how they have dealt with the external barriers you have identified. Next, determine whether you have the resources to implement similar initiatives. If you determine that you do not have the resources, you should seriously reconsider your options. As mentioned above, a community-based social marketing initiative that ignores external barriers is a recipe for failure.

Starting on the next page are some external barriers to sustainable behaviors and some possible solutions.

Examples: Using Convenience to Foster Sustainable Behavior

Agriculture & Conservation

▶ Provide visitors to aquariums with information cards on sustainably harvested seafood that makes it easy for them to identify this seafood when purchasing groceries of eating out. Monterey Bay Aquarium has initiated a successful program that does just that.

Energy

▶ It is inconvenient for homeowners to purchase and install programmable thermostats and other low-cost, quick payback energy efficiency devices. Initiate a door-to-door service that provides and installs these devices.

 Transportation

▶ Commuters often view mass transit as an inconvenient option compared to driving a vehicle. The perceived relative convenience of driving can be altered by making driving less convenient (e.g., slower lane-ways for single-occupant cars, introduce traffic calming and one-way streets).

Waste & Pollution

▶ It is inconvenient to obtain a composting unit. Delivering compost units door-to-door as was done with recycling containers addresses this barrier. When compost units are delivered for free, as they were in a pilot project in the City of Waterloo, Ontario, participation rates can rival those for recycling programs.[10] In that pilot project, a door hanger was distributed to 300 homes informing residents that they had been selected to receive a free composting unit. Of the 300 homes that were contacted, 253 (or 84%) agreed to accept compost units. In a follow-up survey, 77% of these households were found to be using their compost units.

▶ When inconvenience for office recycling is overcome, the effects can be startling. Providing each office worker with a recycling container for fine paper can increase the amount of fine paper retrieved from a few percent to over 75%.

▶ The inconvenience of taking household hazardous waste to a depot results in little of this waste being diverted from the landfill. Providing semi-annual hazardous waste home pick-up dates can dramatically increase proper disposal of this material.

 Water

▶ It is inconvenient to purchase and install toilet dams, faucet aerators and low-flow shower heads. Having home auditors install these devices during home visits addresses these barriers.

Developing Strategies
Revisited

> " *If you only have a hammer, you tend to see every problem as a nail.*
>
> **Abraham Maslow**

The preceding seven chapters introduced a series of behavior change tools that can be incorporated into a community-based social marketing strategy. To showcase how to utilize these tools, a hypothetical program to foster the purchase of products with recycled-content will be introduced. Following this example, elements of effective strategy design will be discussed.

Imagine that barrier and benefit research identified the following barriers to consumers purchasing products that have recycled content: 1) these products are viewed as difficult to identify; 2) shoppers forget to consider whether a product has recycled content; and 3) buying recycled content products is not seen as the "right thing to do." Knowing that recycled-content products are difficult to identify when shopping suggests that prompts could be effective in promoting these purchases. That consumers forget to consider these recycled-content products when making a purchase also suggests that prompts may be an effective tool in promoting the purchase of products with recycled content. Finally, that buying these products is not seen as the "right thing to do" indicates that an effective strategy will need to foster supportive social norms.

What might a community-based social marketing strategy look like which incorporates these behavior change tools? Prompts are most effective when presented at the time an activity is to occur. To encourage the purchase of recycled content products, prompts should be placed on the store shelves directly below these items. To assist shoppers in easily identifying these products, a graphic design that visually suggests the importance of purchasing recycled content products would be used. The prompt would also contain a brief explanation of why buying products with recycled content is important. Remember that for a prompt to be effective, it should contain all of the information that is necessary for someone to act appropriately. Occasionally, it is possible to overcome two barriers to a sustainable behavior with one tool. In this example, prompts make it significantly easier for shoppers to select products that have recycled content, while also increasing the likelihood that shoppers will remember to consider these characteristics when they are shopping.

How might social norms that encourage the purchase of recycled-content products be fostered? Asking shoppers to wear an "I buy recycled" sticker would assist in establishing descriptive social norms as well as enhance commitment to act. Nonetheless, the stickers would only be worn for a short time before being removed. A more permanent way to establish social norms would be to ask shoppers as they enter the store to sign a display in which they commit to purchasing products with recycled content. This display would not only foster the development of social norms, but would also serve as a reminder of their commitment each time they enter the store. Note that these two strategies are not mutually exclusive. We might ask shoppers to wear the sticker for one day in order to build presence for the campaign, while also asking them to sign the display in order to obtain a more permanent commitment. Since people wish to behave consistently, agreeing to wear the sticker and/or sign the display increases the likelihood that they will purchase recycled content products. Furthermore, having check-out clerks utilize injunctive social norms by thanking shoppers for making recycled content purchases would also assist in establishing this norm.

Recall that when developing a social marketing campaign we wish to reduce barriers to the behavior we wish to encourage, while concurrently increasing barriers to the behavior we wish to discourage. The use of the stickers and display will simultaneously lead to the purchase of recycled content products being viewed positively, while the purchase of non-recycled-content products will increasingly meet with social disapproval.

The proposed social marketing strategy deals with each barrier to the purchase of products with recycled content. However, simply selecting and incorporating the tools discussed in this book into a community-based social marketing strategy will not ensure its success. Prior to implementing a strategy broadly, it should be tested through focus groups and a pilot.

ADDRESS BOTH

In developing a community-based social marketing strategy, remember to address both the behavior you wish to encourage and the behavior you wish to discourage.

FOCUS GROUPS

While focus groups can be used to explore barriers to a behavior, they can also provide useful information on the appeal and acceptance of a proposed strategy. To obtain feedback on the above strategy, several focus groups of six to eight individuals would be conducted. For each focus group, the purpose of the campaign would be explained and participants would be introduced to drafts of the proposed prompts, stickers, commitment display sign, and supporting materials such as brochures, posters and an informational video. Focus group participants would be asked whether these materials would capture their attention and if they are clear and easy to understand. Once feedback had been received on the materials, participants would be asked if they perceived any problems with the proposed strategy and if they had any suggestions for how it could be strengthened. Following completion of the focus groups, responses to the program materials and proposed strategies would be tabulated to uncover any themes in participants' responses. Where warranted, the strategy would be refined based on the feedback received. After refining the strategy, the pilot is conducted.

ADDITIONAL THOUGHTS ON DEVELOPING STRATEGIES

When developing a community-based social marketing strategy, keep the following in mind:

1. **SELECT TOOLS BASED ON BARRIERS AND BENEFITS.** Begin by selecting behavior-change tools based on the barriers and benefits that your research has uncovered. In doing this, use the following table for guidance. As the table indicates, if your target audience *lacks motivation*, three tools might be used.

BARRIERS	TOOLS
Lack of Motivation	Commitment Norms Incentives
Forget to Act	Prompts
Lack of Social Pressure	Norms
Lack of Knowledge	Communication Social Diffusion
Structural Barriers	Convenience

Commitments are useful in enhancing motivation when your target audience believes that engaging in the behavior is worthwhile, but they have not yet acted. In contrast, norms can be helpful when your audience does not yet believe it is important to act. Finally, incentives are worth considering when there is little likelihood of the behavior occurring unless motivation is significantly increased. It is worth noting that normally you would not want to use all three of these tools to address the same barrier, as doing so is likely unnecessary and will increase your program delivery costs.

When your target audience *forgets* to engage in the behavior, such as turning off their computer equipment, use prompts. In contrast, if *few people care* whether someone engages in a sustainable behavior this indicates that social norms are not yet operating and should be considered as part of your strategy.

If your target audience lacks knowledge regarding a sustainable behavior, effective communications and social diffusion should be considered. Finally, if *structural barriers* exist to an activity, such as lack of shower facilities for cyclists who ride to work, addressing this barrier will make the behavior more convenient.

This table is not meant to be exhaustive—other barriers to behavioral change exist. It is simply meant to illustrate that for each barrier identified, it will need to be addressed by a behavior change tool.

2. **MAXIMIZE THE EFFECTIVENESS OF TOOLS.** Each behavior change chapter concluded with a checklist for the effective use of the tool covered in that chapter. Use these checklists to ensure that you maximize the impact of these tools.

3. **TACKLE SEVERAL BARRIERS WITH ONE STRATEGY.** Look for the opportunity to tackle several barriers through the use of one strategy. In the chapter on commitment, an anti-idling window sticker was described. This window sticker served as a prompt to remind motorists to turn off their engines, as well as a form of public commitment. However, it also served as a method to develop descriptive norms and foster social diffusion. This one simple sticker, which cost only a few cents per vehicle, had four different behavior change tools built into it.

4. **USE PILOTS TO TEST ONE STRATEGY AGAINST ANOTHER.** If you are uncertain which tool needs to be used, develop several community-based social marketing strategies, with each strategy using a different tool to address the same barrier. This will allow you to assess which of these tools can most effectively address the barrier.

PUBLIC CONSULTATION

Community-based social marketing relies heavily upon public consultation. As noted previously, the process of designing a strategy involves obtaining information from the community at three separate times. First, just after conducting the literature review, focus groups are conducted to obtain in-depth information on barriers and benefits to the behavior you wish to promote. Second, this information is supplemented by a survey, which provides further information about barriers and benefits, attitudes and present levels of involvement in the activity. Third, the proposed community-based social marketing strategy is reviewed in another series of focus groups which provide feedback on the planned strategy. These three steps help ensure that the strategy you devise will be well-tailored to your community.

This consultation should be part of the development of any community-based social marketing strategy. However, you may wish to add another opportunity for public involvement—active participation in determining which behaviors to focus on as well as engagement in developing the community-based social marketing strategy. Some organizations create a stakeholder consultation committee for this purpose. Whether you elect to create a stakeholder consultation committee, and if you do, when they become involved in the process is a matter of personal preference. My own preference is to create a stakeholder committee whenever the planned program is likely to be of special interest or concern (e.g., implementing user fees for garbage disposal), or when the activity you are attempting to promote is not well-understood and hence you need input from as many sources as possible.

If you decide to form a stakeholder committee, it can be formed at the outset (e.g., prior to the literature review), or after information from the literature review, observations, focus groups and survey have been collected and analyzed. Once again, when you decide to form the committee is a matter of personal preference. I prefer to create the committee at the outset if the program has any potential to be controversial in order to circumvent concerns about decisions being made without public input. On the other hand, early creation of the committee can make some initial parts of collecting information on barriers and benefits, such as the survey, torturous if not well-managed. Don't place yourself in the position of writing a survey by committee. Do seek suggestions about potential topics that should be addressed in the survey, but avoid having the survey reviewed by the stakeholder committee.

Independent of when you elect to involve a stakeholder committee, you will need to decide beforehand what constraints will be placed upon the committee. For example, if council has made it clear that no subsidies will be provided for the installation of low-flow toilets, your committee needs to know at the outset what limitations have been placed upon the strategies that can be considered. If you are going to be acting as a facilitator for stakeholder meetings, remain impartial when receiving feedback from participants. Your role is to encourage constructive input on the design of a strategy. Remaining impartial will facilitate receiving the broadest feedback.

The following chapter introduces how to pilot test a community-based social marketing strategy.

Step 4: Piloting

> " *However beautiful the strategy, you*
> *should occasionally look at the results.*
>
> **Winston Churchill**

Think of a pilot as a "test run," an opportunity to work out the bugs before committing to carrying out a strategy broadly. As noted in the chapters on developing strategies, the tools you elect to use in your strategy should be selected based upon the barriers and benefits that you have identified. To pilot the strategy introduced in the previous chapter, store managers of two supermarkets would be approached and asked if they would be willing to participate. The two stores would need to be similar both in the demographics of their shoppers as well as in the products available (two stores of the same chain would be good candidates). By the flip of a coin, one of the stores would be randomly assigned to receive the community-based social marketing strategy, while the other would serve as a comparison or what is referred to as a *control*, and would not receive the strategy.

Prior to piloting the strategy, the rate of purchase for recycled-content products would be determined by examining the computerized inventory records for these items. Note that it is important to collect this data from both stores, since they may differ initially from one another in the rate of purchase for recycled-content items. Also, it is important to obtain this baseline data for a sufficient period of time to ensure that it is indicative of normal purchase habits, rather than seasonal fluctuations. Following this baseline period, the prompts, posters, stickers, pamphlets and video kiosk would be introduced in the intervention store. After introducing the strategy, the rate of purchase of targeted items would be monitored for several months at both stores to ascertain whether the strategy increased the purchase of these products.

To determine whether the strategy alters consumer purchases, the purchase of recycled-content products during the baseline period is compared to purchases during the intervention (seasonal adjustments may need to be made to these numbers to control for increased purchases around events such as Christmas). However, the success of the strategy cannot simply be determined by comparing the purchases of the recycled-content items for the two stores.

The following example clarifies how to correctly determine the impact of the strategy. Imagine that after implementing the above strategy, the intervention store had sold 5000 units of recycled-content toilet paper, while the control store had sold only 3000. On first glance, it appears that the community-based social marketing strategy has brought about a 67% increase in sales for this one item. However, such a conclusion assumes that the stores initially sold an equal amount of recycled-content toilet paper, which is very unlikely. To determine the *real* impact of the intervention, the sales of toilet paper during the baseline period for both stores needs to be considered. Imagine that baseline data revealed that the intervention

LIMIT PILOTS

Never include in a pilot components that you cannot afford to deliver in a broad-scale rollout. Removing these components when moving from a successful pilot to a broad-scale implementation may mean that your broad-scale program fails.

Intervention: 5000-2500 = 2500

Control: 3000-2000 = 1000

Real Impact: 2500-1000 = 1500 (50% increase)

store had sold 2500 units of recycled-content toilet paper in the month prior to the implementing the strategy, and the control store had sold 2000 units. As shown in the preceding table, the real increase in sales that can be attributed to the intervention is 50%.

If, when comparing inventory records prior to and following the implementation of the intervention, little or no change in consumer purchases was observed, then the pilot would need to be revised until significant changes in behavior were found. Since in this strategy the prompts were a central aspect of the campaign, it is natural to start by investigating them. By conducting in-store surveys with a random selection of shoppers, awareness and understanding of the prompts could be probed. If low recognition and understanding of the prompts was found, then the prompts would need to be redesigned to be more prominent and clear. Further, the placement of the posters, that explain the purpose of the prompts, should be examined. Did shoppers recall seeing the posters? Did they know what the posters said? If the answer to either of these questions is "no," it is possible that simply changing the location and/or number of posters might address this problem. Finally, a central element of this community-based social marketing strategy was to foster social norms that support the purchase of recycled-content products. Accordingly, the post-pilot survey should also address whether shoppers believed they should be purchasing recycled-content products. If this is not the case, then the social norm aspects of this program would need to be refined.

The point of a pilot is to identify and address problems before launching a campaign throughout the community. You should plan on there being problems and build into your plans the opportunity to refine your strategy until it works well. On one project, I revised a pilot six times before I was able to produce the desired behavior changes. While it was frustrating to have to make this many revisions, I was thankful that I was making the revisions to a pilot rather than to a larger project, for which the problems would have been much more difficult and expensive to rectify. Expect problems, plan for them; in the end, when you implement community-wide you will be rewarded for the time that you took to troubleshoot your strategy through piloting.

PILOTING PRINCIPLES

Use the following principles as guidelines in conducting a pilot:

1. **DON'T MIX BARRIER AND BENEFIT RESEARCH WITH PILOTING:** It is tempting to use the participants from your barrier and benefit research in a subsequent pilot, but avoid this temptation. The act of participating in focus groups or surveys often leads to greater awareness of the issues you are working on. If you include these people in your pilot, and your pilot is successful, you will not know whether the changes in behavior you observed were due to their participation in the barrier and benefit research, the strategy you employed, or a combination of the two. If the changes are due to either having participated in the barrier and benefit research, or a combination of participating in the barrier and benefit research and your strategy, your program will fail when you move from piloting to broad-scale implementation since these conditions will no longer exist. This concern is greatest when working with small numbers, such as local businesses or farmers in a watershed. In these cases, conduct your barrier and benefit research in similar watersheds or communities in order to avoid the problems noted above.

2. **USE A MINIMUM OF TWO GROUPS TO CONDUCT YOUR PILOT:** When you conduct your pilot, you want to make sure that any changes you observe are the result of your intervention and not other events that are occurring in the community. To be certain that it is your intervention that is bringing about the changes you observe, always include a control group to which no strategy is delivered. By comparing your intervention and control groups, you can be much more confident that your intervention was responsible for any changes you observe. You may wish to have more than two groups. For example, as in many of the studies described in this book, you may wish to have one group receive a commitment strategy, a second receive feedback, a third receive a combination of the two, and a fourth act as a control. Keep in mind that pilots can often be quite inexpensive to conduct since the size of groups can be kept small. Including multiple

groups in your pilot can help you determine the form that your strategy will take when you implement it across your community. For example, as a result of conducting a pilot on fostering car pooling, you may learn that obtaining commitments provides no additional benefit over assisting employees to identify others living in their neighborhood with whom they might drive to work. As a result, your subsequent program would drop commitment as part of the strategy.

3. **USE RANDOM ASSIGNMENT:** When you conduct a pilot, you want to know that the group that receives your intervention is as identical as possible to the group that serves as the control. The only way that you can assure this is if the participants are randomly assigned to one group or another. To randomly assign farmers, businesses, individuals or households to the groups you plan to use, simply place all of their names or addresses in a hat and then pull them out assigning the first selection to the first group, the second to the second group, etc.

4. **MAKE MEASUREMENTS OF BEHAVIOR CHANGE A PRIORITY:** In evaluating the effectiveness of a pilot, your primary concern should always be whether you have been able to change the behavior that you set out to change. Where possible, don't rely upon people's self-reports of their behavior; they can be unreliable. Obtain water records, ask to look in composters, examine weather-stripping, etc. You will also want to examine people's perceptions and attitudes, but don't substitute these for examining actual changes in behavior.

5. **CALCULATE RETURN ON INVESTMENT:** In conducting a community-based social marketing pilot, we want to know that not only have we effectively changed behavior, but that we have done so cost-effectively. To calculate return on investment, follow these guidelines from Nancy Lee:[1] (see next page)

A. Dollars Spent: Includes all costs associated with developing and conducting the pilot.

B. Behaviors Influenced: Number of people who engaged in the targeted behavior.

C. Cost per Behavior Influenced: Divide Dollars Spent (A) by Behaviors Influenced (B).

D. Benefit per Behavior: Costs avoided, such as health care costs, by encouraging more active forms of transportation. Avoided costs can at times be difficult to estimate.

To calculate return on investment:
Step 1: Gross Economic Benefit = B * D
Step 2: Net Benefit = Gross Economic Benefit - A
Step 3: ROI = (Net Benefit/A)*100

It is worth noting that the rate of behavioral change is not the only determinant of what program you might implement across a community. By calculating return on investment, you might learn that one behavior change strategy results in only a slight lower adoption rate of the behavior than a more expensive strategy, but at only a fraction of the cost.

6. **REVISE YOUR PILOT UNTIL IT IS EFFECTIVE:** It is tempting when a pilot is ineffective to assume that you know what went wrong and to move directly to community-wide implementation. Keep in mind that pilots can often be conducted very quickly. Take the time to run another pilot to confirm that you are actually able to change behavior before you implement across a community. The extra time that you take to run the pilot may save you hundreds of thousands of dollars and, possibly, your job.

Step 5: Broad-scale Implementation and Evaluation

" *Always remember that the future comes one day at a time.*

Dean Acheson

When a pilot has demonstrated that a behavioral change can be brought about cost-effectively, it is time to broadly implement the strategy. Prior to broad-scale implementation, collect baseline information regarding the present level of engagement in the behavior to be promoted. Where possible, use actual observations of behavior or reliable records (e.g., water meter readings) rather than self-reports to establish this baseline. Once you have implemented your program, begin to collect data to ascertain its impact. Keep in mind that you will want to conduct these evaluations at different time intervals in order to assess whether your behavioral change strategy is having a long-term impact. It is common with repetitive behavioral changes, such as recycling, for engagement in the behavior to trail off. Ongoing evaluation will allow you to detect these changes and implement programs to counter them.

In implementing the strategy broadly, advertising and local media can be used to create additional awareness that would have been undesirable during the pilot. In implementing an initiative throughout a community, limited advertising resources can be leveraged by creating public awareness through hosting media events to both launch the campaign and provide feedback on its success.

How would the buy-recycled campaign, introduced in the two previous chapters, be evaluated were it to be implemented broadly? A random selection of participating retailers would be chosen to participate in the evaluation. Baseline data from the electronic inventories of these stores would be obtained and then compared to changes that occurred in the purchase of the recycled-content products following the launch of the campaign. To provide an overall picture of the impact this campaign had upon the purchase of these products, the average increase in the purchase of these products across all product categories and evaluation stores would be determined. This information not only serves as a critical test of the success of the initiative, but serves two other important functions. First, it is important to provide the individuals who shop at these stores with feedback regarding the impact that purchases have upon the environment. In other words, an element of a successful community-based social marketing strategy is providing feedback that reinforces changes that people have made. The media will often provide you with a cost-effective way of getting this information back to consumers, though other possibilities exist. One vivid and ongoing form of feedback is to provide shoppers in each retail store with a yardstick of their efforts. By setting up a display in which the percentage increase in the purchase of these products is updated on a regular basis, shoppers can be provided with an ongoing source of feedback and encouragement (the use of this form of feedback can also help to further establish a social norm regarding the purchase of recycled-content products). Second, program evaluation provides evidence of concrete results, which will assist you in convincing funding agencies that your campaign deserves continued support.

PROVIDE FEEDBACK

Providing feedback about a program's success reinforces the behavioral changes that people have made. This is particularly important when the behavioral change is repetitive and when meaningful impact can only be obtained when numerous people engage in the action.

GUIDELINES FOR SELECTING CONSULTANTS

You may wish to contract out the design, implementation and evaluation of your program. Here are some suggestions to increase the likelihood that you ultimately choose a firm with the necessary skills to use community-based social marketing. In the request for proposals, ask that submissions:

▸ be based upon community-based social marketing methods;

▸ specify how behaviors will be selected;

▸ specify how barriers and benefits will be identified;

▸ clarify what behavior change tools might be used (e.g., commitment, prompts, norms, social diffusion, etc.);

▸ indicate how the strategy will be piloted;

▸ specify how the program will be evaluated once implemented throughout the community;

▸ provide evidence of competence in survey design, program evaluation and data analysis (at least one member of the research team should have graduate level training in research methods and statistics); and

▸ provide evidence of familiarity with designing and implementing community-based social marketing strategies.

SHARING KNOWLEDGE
Use the discussion forums on the Fostering Sustainable Behavior website to let others know of programs that you have pilot tested or implemented broadly (cbsm.com).

THE FINAL REPORT: GETTING THE WORD OUT

After conducting a literature review; observations; focus groups; writing, conducting and analyzing a survey; devising a strategy; scrutinizing it with focus groups and a stakeholder committee; piloting the strategy; revising the strategy; implementing it throughout the community; and evaluating it, you should be finished, right? Wrong. Community-based social marketing is an emerging field that holds great promise for moving us toward a sustainable future. Take the time to write up a final report and make sure that people know about it via the discussion forums on our website. Whether your community-based social marketing strategy was successful or not, others need to learn from your efforts.

Concluding Thoughts

> *" The difference between what we do and what we are capable of doing would suffice to solve most of the world's problems.*
>
> **Mohandas K. Gandhi**

A colleague of mine, who designs waste-reduction strategies for a regional municipality, told me that while he was reading the first edition of this book he grew increasingly uncomfortable. His discomfort, he explained, came from realizing that the tools and strategies set out here are more effective than the ones he was using presently, and that he would have to change how he designed and delivered programs. He went on to explain that he had grown comfortable with the tools that he had used for some time and that using community-based social marketing would involve relearning important aspects of his job. Resistance to using community-based social marketing, he correctly pointed out, has to be overcome even by those who believe in its utility.

OVERCOMING RESISTANCE IN YOURSELF

Clearly, the tools and strategies detailed in this book will initially require more work. Implementing a community-based social marketing strategy requires careful preliminary research, strategy development, piloting, implementation and evaluation. However, this attention to detail is in large part why community-based social marketing is often so successful. Following the steps described here can greatly increase the likelihood of your program working. For example: the literature review allows your program to build on the work of others; the observations, focus groups and survey allow you to determine what barriers and benefits will need to be addressed in order to design an effective community-based social marketing strategy; piloting the strategy will allow you to test its impact and further refine the strategy to increase its effectiveness; and evaluating the program once it has been implemented across the community will allow you to speak with confidence regarding its impact and provide you with the data you need to ensure continued funding.

Program design and evaluation are critical components of community-based social marketing, but they are not unique to it. Increasingly, program design and evaluation are being mandated for a wide range of social programs. As governments are increasingly held accountable for the wise use of tax dollars, program design and evaluation will become the norm rather than the exception. Further, over time, program design and evaluation reduce the cost and effort that has to be expended to foster sustainable behavior. Programs that are not properly designed and evaluated are frequently less effective. As a consequence, several programs often have to be developed and delivered to bring about the same change in behavior as one well-designed program. In short, properly designing and evaluating a community-based social marketing strategy will initially entail more work on your part, but this effort will be rewarded both through greater impact and lower long-term costs.

OVERCOMING RESISTANCE AMONG COLLEAGUES

The approaches detailed in this book may be seen as unproven by your colleagues. How can you overcome their resistance? It will help if you prepare for some of the problems that you might encounter.

You will need to be prepared to deal with concerns your colleagues will have over the length of time that it will take to design and implement a community-based social marketing strategy. You will need to reassure them that the approaches outlined here are more likely to succeed, and as a result, resources and staff will be used more responsibly and effectively. Additionally, be prepared that some of your colleagues may not want to evaluate programs for fear that evaluation might produce negative results. You may also encounter resistance to community-based social marketing since using these approaches may be seen by some colleagues as an implicit admission that past initiatives were not designed as effectively as they might have been.

Here are some suggestions for increasing support for community-based social marketing in your organization: ask colleagues to read this book; bring in a speaker to introduce community-based social marketing to your organization or make a presentation yourself (you'll find a presentation that you can download for free, along with speaking notes, in the resources section of the cbsm.com website); distribute articles that demonstrate the effectiveness of community-based social marketing strategies; ask someone who has successfully implemented a community-based social marketing strategy to come and speak to your organization about it; ask that current programs be rigorously evaluated and that the evaluation focus on behavior change rather than awareness of marketing messages. It is easy to believe that a program is working if little or no concrete data exists to measure its success.

Be prepared that it may take a considerable length of time to overcome resistance from your colleagues. Indeed, you may put forward several community-based social marketing proposals only to find each of them rejected. Remember, as you advocate with resistant colleagues, you are slowly creating new norms regarding how programs should be carried out. You can be confident that eventually community-based social marketing strategies will replace the more traditional approaches discussed in the first chapter for one simple reason: They are more effective.

MEETING THE CHALLENGE

As we move rapidly toward a world with nine billion inhabitants, and ever dwindling renewable resources, the tools and methods described here will become increasingly important. Community-based social marketing holds great promise in promoting sustainable behavior, but we have failed to date to put in place the structures that would enable many to make most effective use of this process. Below are several recommendations to address these shortcomings.

1. **TIER BEHAVIORS:** At present, there is a lack of rigorous information regarding which behaviors are most important to target. There is a clear role for federal/state/provincial (FSP) agencies to collect this information and make it accessible to those who work at the local level to deliver environmental behavioral change programs. Without a coordinated FSP effort to collect this information, local agencies will continue to guess regarding which behavioral changes are the most important to foster. I recommend that for each domain and sector, such as residential energy, behaviors should be tiered. Tier one would include those behaviors that have the best combination of high impact and probability, and low penetration. Tier two would consist of those behaviors, that while less important than tier one, are nevertheless worth pursuing once we have adequately addressed tier one behaviors. Finally, tier three behaviors are those actions that we would only elect to pursue once we had exhausted promoting tier one, and then tier two, behaviors. It is recommended that national online repositories be created that allow local agencies to quickly determine which behaviors in their region are the most worthwhile to foster.

2. **PROVIDE BARRIER AND BENEFIT RESEARCH:** In addition to tiering behaviors, FSP agencies have a role to play in conducting and disseminating barrier and benefit research. Currently, local agencies conduct their own research, if they conduct barrier and benefit research at all. With many local agencies working on the same behavioral changes, such as encouraging bicycling, not only is this a massive duplication of effort, but often this work is conducted with inadequate resources. It is far more sensible to have this research coordinated at the FSP level, provided that it is conducted in such a way that the research speaks to potential differences in barriers and benefits that may exist for different communities or regions.

3. **INITIATE TWO-STAGE FUNDING:** If we want local organizations to follow a community-based social marketing process, funding agencies need to explicitly support pilots preceding broad-scale implementations. In addition to supporting pilots, careful attention needs to be given to the development of the strategies to be pilot-tested. Since programs that directly address the barriers to, and benefits of, a behavioral change are more likely to be successful, FSP agencies should require that applications for funding show a clear correspondence between the strategy being recommended and the barrier and benefit research.

4. **PROVIDE TURNKEY PROGRAMS:** Most local agencies are working on very similar behavioral change programs. For example, efforts to increase energy efficiency, reduce waste, alter transportation habits, increase water efficiency and protect watersheds abound. In those cases in which the barriers and benefits to a behavioral change have been found to be common across different communities, FSP agencies should pilot-test promising community-based social marketing strategies in several jurisdictions. When found to be effective, turnkey programs should be created and web-hosted so that local agencies can easily access them. Initiatives—such as Natural Resources Canada's Turn it Off program, featured in the chapter on commitment—demonstrate just how effective turnkey programs can be in fostering the rapid deployment of effective strategies.

5. **HIRE COMMUNITY-BASED SOCIAL MARKETERS:** Many local agencies do not have the resources to hire community-based social marketing staff. To assist them with developing more effective programs, FSP agencies should provide access to community-based social marketers who can help local agencies with the development of their strategies. This one recommendation could significantly improve the quality of local behavioral change programs.

6. **PROVIDE COMMUNITY-BASED SOCIAL MARKETING TRAINING:** The most frequent question that I am asked when I deliver workshops is, "How can I learn more?" At present, there are no undergraduate or graduate programs that provide extensive training in community-based social marketing. There is a desperate need for FSP agencies to work with universities in providing this training.

7. **VISION SUSTAINABILITY:** To date, we have failed to provide a clear vision of how a sustainable future is preferable to our present. A colleague, Robert Olson, once wrote, "All the other influences shaping society can themselves be influenced by changes in our assumptions about what is possible and changes in our aspirations for what we want the future to be like." (p. 16).[1] In failing to articulate the desirability of a sustainable future we have undermined our very ability to achieve it. As a consequence, our various programs to foster sustainable behavior sit divorced from the broader vision they are meant to serve. Given the plethora of environmental crises humanity faces, FSP agencies have a moral responsibility to respond to these crises with clear and inspiring visions of a sustainable future and how these disparate programs serve that common purpose.

GOING FORWARD

The speed with which community-based social marketing supplants less-effective traditional approaches will depend upon the quick dissemination of our successes and failures in using this approach. The adoption of new techniques, such as community-based social marketing, occurs primarily through the informal sharing of information. I encourage you to actively discuss your efforts in using these new techniques with others, and to make use of the on-line discussion forums at the Fostering Sustainable Behavior website (cbsm.com). Through the forums, you have the opportunity to share your successes and failures in the use of community-based social marketing, and to learn from the experiences of others who are tackling similar problems. Each time we share information and refine our techniques, we collectively become a little wiser and move a step closer to the sustainable future our children deserve.

Acknowledgements

Over the past twenty-five years I have discussed the ideas of community-based social marketing with thousands of environmental program planners. These conversations have strongly influenced all three editions of this book. Thank you for your work—it is an inspiration and a comfort.

I would also like to acknowledge the contributions that many authors have made to the ideas expressed in this book. Foremost among these is the work of Gerry Gardner and Paul Stern (see their ground-breaking book, *Environmental Problems and Human Behavior*), Philip Kotler and Nancy Lee (see their influential book, *Social Marketing*) and William Smith, who coauthored the second edition with me. I have also been influenced by the writings of Jan Aceti, Alan Andreasen, Eliot Aronson, Shawn Burn, Robert Cialdini, Mark Costanzo, John Darley, Scott Geller, Marti Hope Gonzales, William Kempton, Ed Maibach, Wesley Schultz, Clive Seligman, Deborah Winter,

Neil Wolman, and Ray de Young, among others. I would like to personally thank James Dyal and Stuart Oskamp, two mentors, who encouraged my interest in applying psychology to sustainability.

I would particularly like to thank my Canadian colleagues, Dave Dilks, Dan Dolderman, Ken Donnelly, Jay Kassirer, Jenn Lynes and Manuel Reimer, with whom I have spent numerous hours discussing how best to advance the use of community-based social marketing.

Justin Kuntz and Brian Loomis are responsible for the remarkable website that supports and extends this book. Justin Kuntz and Steve Norell, of Creative Soapbox, designed the cover and layout for this new edition, and Sue McKenzie-Mohr and Louise Fraser patiently coaxed me through the finer aspects of the English language. Thanks also to New Society, a terrific publisher, who *walks the talk*. I encourage you to explore their other offerings.

Finally, my wife, Sue, and my daughters, Jaime and Taryn, have supported not only this book, but a life spent wandering to promote the use of community-based social marketing. I'm fortunate to have the support and love of three such wonderful women.

References

FOSTERING SUSTAINABLE BEHAVIOR

1. Bem, D.J. (1972). "Self-perception theory." In L. Berkowitz (Ed.), *Advances in Experimental Social Psychology* (Vol. 6, pp. 63-108). New York: Academic.

2. Dietz, T., Gardner, G.T., Gilligan, J., Stern, P., & Vandenbergh, M.P. (2009). "Household actions can provide a behavioral wedge to rapidly reduce US carbon emissions." *Proceedings of the National Academy of Sciences, 106(44)*, 18452-18456.

3. Geller, E.S. (1981). "Evaluating energy conservation programs: Is verbal report enough?" *Journal of Consumer Research*, 8, 331-335.

4. Midden, C. J., Meter, J. E., Weenig, M. H., & Zieverink, H. J. (1983). "Using feedback, reinforcement and information to reduce energy consumption in households: A field-experiment." *Journal of Economic Psychology*, 3, 65-86.

5. Jordan, J. R., Hungerford, H. R., & Tomera, A. N. (1986). "Effects of two residential environmental workshops on high school students." *Journal of Environmental Education, 18,* 15-22.

6. Geller, E. S., Erickson, J. B., & Buttram, B. A. (1983). "Attempts to promote residential water conservation with educational, behavioral and engineering strategies." *Population and Environment, 6,* 96-112.

7. Environment Canada. (2006). *Evaluation of the one-tonne challenge program.* Available online at: http://www.ec.gc. ca/ae-ve/F2F5FD59-3DDA-46BC-A62E-C29FDD61E2C5/ EvaluationReport-OTC-Eng.doc.

8. Tedeschi, R. G., Cann, A., & Siegfried, W. D. (1982). "Participation in voluntary auto emissions inspection." *Journal of Social Psychology, 117,* 309-310.

9. Bickman, L. (1972). "Environmental attitudes and actions." *Journal of Social Psychology, 87,* 323-324.

10. Finger, M. (1994). "From knowledge to action? Exploring the relationships between environmental experiences, learning, and behavior." *Journal of Social Issues, 50,* 141-160.

11. Archer, D., Pettigrew, T., Costanzo, M., Iritani, B., Walker, I. & White, L. (1987). "Energy conservation and public policy: The mediation of individual behavior." Energy Efficiency: *Perspectives on Individual Behavior,* 69-92.

12. De Young, R. (1989). "Exploring the difference between recyclers and non-recyclers: The role of information." *Journal of Environmental Systems, 18,* 341-351.

13. Costanzo, M., Archer, D., Aronson, E., & Pettigrew, T. (1986). "Energy conservation behavior: The difficult path from information to action." *American Psychologist, 41,* 521-528.

14. Hirst, E. (1984). "Household energy conservation: A review of the federal residential conservation service." *Public Administration Review, 44,* 421-430.

15. Hirst, E., Berry, L., & Soderstrom, J. (1981). "Review of utility home energy audit programs." *Energy, 6,* 621-630.

16. Hirst, E. (1984). "Household energy conservation: A review of the federal residential conservation service." *Public Administration Review, 44,* 421-430.

17. Stern, P.C., & Aronson, E. (Eds.). (1984). *"Energy use: The human dimension."* New York: Freeman.

18. Larson, M. A. & Massetti-Miller, K. L. (1984). "Measuring change after a public education campaign." *Public Relations Review, 10,* 23-32.

19. Pope, E. (1982, December 10). "PG&E's loans aimed at poor miss the mark." San Jose *Mercury*, p. 6B.

20. Costanzo, M., Archer, D., Aronson, E., & Pettigrew, T. (1986). "Energy conservation behavior: The difficult path from information to action. *American Psychologist,"* 41, 521-528.

21. Costanzo, M., Archer, D., Aronson, E., & Pettigrew, T. (1986). "Energy conservation behavior: The difficult path from information to action." *American Psychologist, 41,* 521-528.

22. Stern, P.C., & Oskamp, S. (1987). "Managing scarce environmental resources." In D. Stokols, & I. Altman (Eds.), *Handbook of Environmental Psychology (pp. 1043-1088).* New York: Wiley.

23. McKenzie-Mohr, D., Nemiroff, L. S., Beers, L., & Desmarais, S. (1995). "Determinants of responsible environmental behavior." *Journal of Social Issues, 51,* 139-156.

24. Oskamp, S., Harrington, M.J., Edwards, T.C., Sherwood, D.L., Okuda, S.M., & Swanson, D.C. (1991). "Factors influencing household recycling behavior." *Environment and Behavior, 23,* 494-519; and Tracy, A.P., & Oskamp, S. (1983-84). "Relationships among ecologically responsible behaviors." *Journal of Environmental Systems, 13,* 115-126.

STEP 1: SELECTING BEHAVIORS

1. Natural Resources Canada (2010). *Canada's secondary energy use by sector, end-use and sub-sector.* Available online at: http://oee.nrcan-rncan.gc.ca/corporate/statistics/neud/dpa/tableshandbook2/aaa_ca_2_e_4.cfm?attr=0

2. Hargroves, K., Desha, C. & McKenzie-Mohr, D. (2009). Personal communication.

3. Natural Resources Canada (2010). *Total end-use sector. Energy use analysis.* Available online at: http://oee.nrcan-rncan.gc.ca/corporate/statistics/neud/dpa/tablesanalysis2/aaa_ca_1_e_4.cfm?attr=0

STEP 2: IDENTIFYING BARRIERS AND BENEFITS

1. See, for example, Sudman, S. & Bradburn, N.M. (1982). *Asking questions: A practical guide to questionnaire design.* San Francisco: Jossey-Bass.
2. Fowler, Jr., F. J. (1984). *Survey research methods.* Beverly Hills, CA: Sage, p. 101.
3. McKenzie-Mohr, D., Nemiroff, L.S., Beers, L. & Desmarais, S. (1995). "Determinants of responsible environmental behavior." *Journal of Social Issues, 51,* 139-156.

COMMITMENT

1. Freedman, J.L., & Fraser, S. C. (1966). "Compliance without pressure: The foot-in-the-door technique." *Journal of Personality and Social Psychology, 4,* 195-202.
2. Freedman, J.L., & Fraser, S. C. (1966). "Compliance without pressure: The foot-in-the-door technique." *Journal of Personality and Social Psychology, 4,* 195-202.
3. Schwarzwald, J., Raz, M., & Zvibel, M. (1979). "The efficacy of the door-in-the-face technique when established behavioral customs exist." *Journal of Applied Social Psychology, 9,* 576-586.
4. Sherman, S. J. (1980). "On the self-erasing nature of errors of prediction." *Journal of Personality and Social Psychology, 39,* 211-221.
5. Greenwald, A.G., Carnot, C.G., Beach, R., & Young, B. (1987). "Increasing voting behavior by asking people if they expect to vote." *Journal of Applied Psychology, 72,* 315-318.
6. Lipsitz, A., Kallmeyer, K., Ferguson, M., & Abas, A. (1989). "Counting on blood donors: Increasing the impact of reminder calls." *Journal of Applied Social Psychology, 19,* 1057-1067.
7. Pliner, P., Hart, H., Kohl, J., & Saari, D. (1974). "Compliance without pressure: Some further data on the foot-in-the-door technique." *Journal of Experimental Social Psychology, 10,* 17-22.

8.   Boyce, T. E. & Geller, E.S. (2000). "A community-wide intervention to improve pedestrian safety: Guidelines for institutionalizing large-scale behavior change." *Environment and Behavior, 32(4),* 502-520.

9.   Burger, J.M. (2000). "The foot in the door compliance procedure: A multiple-process analysis and review." *Personality and Social Psychology Review, 3(4),* 303-325.

10. Michel-Guillou, E. & Moser, G. (2006). "Commitment of farmers to environmental protection: From social pressure to environmental conscience." *Journal of Environmental Psychology, 26,* 227-235.

11. Bem, D.J. (1972). "Self-perception theory." In L. Berkowitz (Ed.), *Advances in Experimental Social Psychology (Vol. 6, pp. 63-108).* New York: Academic.

12. Cialdini, R. B. (1993). *Influence: Science and practice.* New York, NY: HarperCollins College Publishers.

13. Moriarty, T. (1975). "Crime, commitment, and the responsive bystander." *Journal of Personality and Social Psychology, 31,* 370-376.

14. Gonzales, M.H., Aronson, E., & Costanzo, M.A. (1988). "Using social cognition and persuasion to promote energy conservation: A quasi-experiment." *Journal of Applied Social Psychology, 18,* 1049-1066.

15. Shippee, G. E., & Gregory, W. L. (1982). "Public commitment and energy conservation." *American Journal of Community Psychology, 10,* 81-93.

16. Phase 5 Consulting Group (1998). *Research related to behavior that impacts fuel consumption.* Natural Resources Canada: Ottawa, Canada.

17. McKenzie-Mohr & Associates & Lura Consulting (2001). *Turn it Off: Reducing vehicle engine idling.* Environment Canada.

18. Natural Resources Canada (2010). *Toward and idle-free nation: The evolution of Canada's idle-free initiative.* Natural Resources Canada: Ottawa, Canada.

19. Hutton, R.R. (1982). Advertising and the Department of Energy's campaign for energy conservation. *Journal of Advertising, 11,* 27-39.

20. Werner, C. M., Turner, J., Shipman, K., Twitchell, F. S., et al. (1995). "Commitment, behavior, and attitude change: An analysis of voluntary recycling." Special Issue: Green psychology. *Journal of Environmental Psychology*, 15, 197-208.

21. Lokhorst, A.M., van Dijk, J., Staats, H., van Dijk, E & de Snoo, G. (2010). "Using tailored information and public commitment to improve the environmental quality of farm lands: An example from the Netherlands." *Human Ecology, 38,* 113–122

22. Pardini, A.U., & Katzev, R.D. (1983-84). "The effects of strength of commitment on newspaper recycling." *Journal of Environmental Systems, 13, 245-254.*

23. Pallak, M.S., Cook, D.A., & Sullivan, J.J. (1980). "Commitment and energy conservation." In L. Bickman (Ed.), *Applied Social Psychology Annual* (pp. 235-253). Beverly Hills, CA: Sage.

24. Wang, T. H. & Katzev, R. D. (1990). "Group commitment and resource conservation: Two field experiments on promoting recycling." *Journal of Applied Social Psychology,* 20, 265-275.

25. Gonzales, M.H., Aronson, E., & Costanzo, M.A. (1988). "Using social cognition and persuasion to promote energy conservation: A quasi-experiment." *Journal of Applied Social Psychology,* 18, 1049-1066.

26. Stern, P.C., & Gardner, G.T. (1981). "Psychological research and energy policy." *American Psychologist,* 36, 329-342.

27. Burn, S.M., & Oskamp, S. (1986). "Increasing community recycling with persuasive communication and public commitment." *Journal of Applied Social Psychology,* 16, 29-41.

28. Burn, S.M. (1991). "Social psychology and the stimulation of recycling behaviors: The block leader approach." *Journal of Applied Social Psychology,* 21, 611-629.

29. Kraut, R. E. (1973). "Effects of social labeling on giving to charity." *Journal of Experimental Social Psychology,* 9, 551-562.

SOCIAL NORMS

1. Asch, S. (1951). "Effects of group pressure upon the modification and distortion of judgment." In M. H. Guetzkow (Ed.), *Groups, leadership and men (pp. 117-190)*. Pittsburgh: Carnegie.; and Asch, S. (1956). "Studies of independence and conformity: A minority of one against a unanimous majority." *Psychological Monographs, 70 (9, Whole No. 416)*.

2. Aronson, E., & O'Leary, M. (1982-83). "The relative effectiveness of models and prompts on energy conservation: A field experiment in a shower room." *Journal of Environmental Systems, 12*, 219-224.

3. Cialdini, R.B., Reno, R.R., & Kallgren, C.A. (1990). "A focus theory of normative conduct: Recycling the concept of norms to reduce littering in public places." *Journal of Personality and Social Psychology, 58*, 1015-1026.

4. Cialdini, R.B. (2003). "Crafting normative messages to protect the environment." *Current Directions in Psychological Science.* 105-109.

6. Goldstein, N.J., Griskevicius, V., & Cialdini, R.B. (2007). "Invoking social norms: A social psychology perspective on improving hotel's linen-reuse programs." *Cornell Hotel and Restaurant Administration Quarterly, 48(2)*, 145-150.

5. Cialdini, R.B., Demaine, L.J., Sagarin, B.J., Barret, D.W., Rhoads, K. & Winter, P.L. (2006). "Managing social norms for persuasive impact." *Social Influence, 1(1)*, 3-15.

7. Griskevicius, V.G., Cialdini, R.B., & Goldstein, N.H. (2008). "Social norms: An underestimated and underemployed lever for managing climate change." *International Journal of Sustainability Communication*, 5-13.

8. Cialdini, R.B., Demaine, L.J., Sagarin, B.J., Barret, D.W., Rhoads, K. & Winter, P.L. (2006). "Managing social norms for persuasive impact." *Social Influence, 1(1)*, 3-15.

9. Schultz, P.W., Nolan, J.M., Cialdini, R.B., Goldstein, N.J., & Griskevikius, V. (2007). "The constructive, destructive, and reconstructive power of social norms." *Psychological Science, 18 (5)*, 429-434.

10. Ayres, I., Raseman, S., & Shih, A. (2009). *Evidence from two large field experiments that peer comparison feedback can reduce residential energy usage*. National Bureau of Economic Research (Report 15386).

11. Hunt, A. (2010). *Social Norms and Energy Conservation*. Cambridge, MA: Massachusetts Institute of Technology, Center for Energy and Environmental Policy Research.

12. Hopper, J. R., & Nielsen, J. M. (1991). "Recycling as altruistic behavior: Normative and behavioral strategies to expand participation in a community recycling program." *Environment and Behavior, 23,* 195-220.

13. Grasmick, H.G., Bursik Jr., R. B. & Kinsey, K.A. (1991). "Shame and embarrassment as deterrents to noncompliance with the law: The case of the antilittering campaign." *Environment and Behavior, 22,* 233-251.

14. Aronson, E., & O'Leary, M. (1982-83). "The relative effectiveness of models and prompts on energy conservation: A field experiment in a shower room." *Journal of Environmental Systems, 12,* 219-224.

SOCIAL DIFFUSION

1. Rogers, E.M. (2003). *Diffusion of Innovations (5th ed.)*. New York: Free Press.

2. Aronson, E. & Gonzales, M. H. (1990). "Alternative social influence processes applied to energy conservation." In J. Edwards, R.S. Tindale, L. Heath & E. J. Posaval (Ed.). *Social influences processes and prevention. (pp. 301-325)*. New York: Plenum.

3. Ester, P. & Winett, R. A. (1982). "Toward more effective antecedent strategies for environmental programs." *Journal of Environmental Systems, 11, 3,* 201-221.

4. Aronson, E. & Gonzales, M. H. (1990). "Alternative social influence processes applied to energy conservation." In J. Edwards, R.S. Tindale, L. Heath & E. J. Posaval (Ed.). *Social influences processes and prevention. (pp. 301-325)*. New York: Plenum.

5. Rogers, E.M. (2003). *Diffusion of Innovations (5th ed.)*. New York: Free Press.

6. Darley, J.M. (1977-78). "Energy conservation techniques as innovations, and their diffusion." *Energy and Buildings, 1,* 339-343.

7. Leonard-Barton, D. (1980). *The role of interpersonal communication networks in the diffusion of energy conserving practices and technologies.* Banff, Alberta, Canada: Consumer Behavior and Energy Use.

8. Oskamp, S., Harrington, M. J., Edwards, T. C., Sherwood, D. L., Okuda, S. M., & Swanson, D. C. (1991). "Factors influencing household recycling behavior." *Environment and Behavior, 23,* 4, 494-519.

9. Rogers, E.M. (2003). *Diffusion of Innovations (5th ed.).* New York: Free Press.

10. LaBay, D. G., & Kinnear, T. C. (1981). "Exploring the consumer decision process in the adoption of solar energy systems." *Journal of Consumer Research, 8(3),* 271-278.

11. Smith, W. (2004) "Ev Rogers: Helping to build a modern synthesis." *Journal of Health Communication, 9,* 139-142.

12. Ostlund, L. (1974). "Perceived innovation attributes as predictors of innovativeness." *Journal of Consumer Research, 1,* 23-29.

13. Ester, P. & Winett, R. A. (1982). "Toward more effective antecedent strategies for environmental programs." *Journal of Environmental Systems, 11,* 3, 201-221.

14. Cobern, M. K., Porter, B.E., Leeming, F.C., & Dwyer, W.O. (1995). "The effect of commitment on adoption and diffusion of grass cycling." Special Issue: Litter control and recycling. *Environment and Behavior, 27* (2), 213-232.

15. Contact Su Beran at the Minnesota Office of Environmental Assistance for more information (su.beran@moea.state.mn.us). This write-up is based on report prepared by Su Beran and April McGrath for the Fostering Sustainable Behavior website.

16. Tyson, B., Worthley, T. & Danley, K. (2004). "Layering Natural Resource and Human Resource data for Planning Watershed Conservation Campaigns." *Society and Natural Resources. 17(2),* 163-170.

PROMPTS

1. Gardner, G. T. & Stern, P.C. (1996). *Environmental problems and human behavior.* Boston: Allyn and Bacon.

2. Kurz, T., Donaghue, N. & Walker, I. (2005). "Utilizing a social-ecological framework to promote water and energy conservation: A field experiment." *Journal of Applied Social Psychology, 35(6),* 1281-1300.

3. de Kort, Y.A., McCalley, L.T. & Midden, C.J. (2008). "Persuasive trash cans: Activation of littering norms by design." *Environment and Behavior, 40(6),* 870-891.

4. Duffy, S. & Verges, M. (2009). "It matters a hole lot: Perceptual affordances of waste containers influence recycling compliance." *Environment and Behavior, 41(5),* 741-749.

5. Smith, J. M., & Bennett, R. (1992). "Several antecedent strategies in the reduction of an environmentally destructive behavior." *Psychological Reports, 70,* 241-242.

6. Jason, L. A., Zolik, E. S., & Matese, F. J. (1979). "Prompting dog owners to pick up dog droppings." *American Journal of Community Psychology, 7(3),* 339-351.

7. O'Neill, G. W., Blanck, L. S., & Joyner, M. A. (1980). "The use of stimulus control over littering in a natural setting." *Journal of Applied Behavior Analysis, 13,* 379-381.

8. Geller, E. S., Brasted, W. S., & Mann, M. F. (1979). "Waste receptacle designs as interventions for litter control." *Journal of Environmental Systems, 9,* 145-160.

9. Luyben, P. D. (1984). "Drop and tilt: A comparison of two procedures to increase the use of venetian blinds to conserve energy." *Journal of Community Psychology, 12,* 149-154.

10. Luyben, P. & Cummings, S. (1981-82). "Motivating beverage container recycling on a college campus." *Journal of Environmental Systems, 11,* 235-245.

11. Houghton, S. (1993). "Using verbal and visual prompts to control littering in high schools." *Educational Studies, 19,* 247-254.

12. Austin, J., Hatfield, D. B., Grindle, A. C. & Bailey, J. S. (1993). "Increasing recycling in office environments: The effects of specific, informative cues." *Journal of Applied Behavior Analysis, 26,* 247-253.

13. Schwartz, J. (1990). "Shopping for a model community." *Garbage, May-June,* 35-38.

14. To obtain more information about this initiative, contact the Central States Education Center, 809 South Fifth St., Champaign, Illinois 61820, (217) 344 2371.

15. Herrick, D. (1995). "Taking it to the stores: Retail sales of recycled products." *Resource Recycling.*

16. For additional information regarding the "Get in the Loop - Buy Recycled" campaign, contact: King County Commission for Marketing Recyclable Materials, 400 Yesler Way, Suite 200, Seattle, Washington, 98104, (206) 296 4439.

17. Bach, C. (2000). *Outdoor residential water reduction programs: Do they really work?* Unpublished report.

COMMUNICATION

1. Stern, P.C., & Aronson, E. (Ed.). (1984). *Energy use: The human dimension.* New York: Freeman.

2. Gonzales, M.H., Aronson, E., & Costanzo, M.A. (1988). "Using social cognition and persuasion to promote energy conservation: A quasi-experiment." *Journal of Applied Social Psychology, 18,* 1049-1066.

3. Gonzales, M.H., Aronson, E., & Costanzo, M.A. (1988). "Using social cognition and persuasion to promote energy conservation: A quasi-experiment." *Journal of Applied Social Psychology, 18,* 1049-1066.

4. Burn, S.M. (1991). "Social psychology and the stimulation of recycling behaviors: The block leader approach." *Journal of Applied Social Psychology, 21,* 611-629.

5. Kempton, W., & Montgomery, L. (1982). "Folk quantification of energy." *Energy, 10,* 817-827.

6. Kempton, W., Harris, C.K., Keith, J.G., & Weihl, J.S. (1984). "Do consumers know what works in energy conservation?" In J. Harris & C. Blumstein (Eds.), *What works: Documenting energy conservation in buildings (pp. 429-438)*. Washington, D.C.: American Council for an Energy Efficient Economy.

7. Kempton, W., & Montgomery, L. (1982). "Folk quantification of energy." *Energy, 10*, 817-827.

8. Eagly, A.H., & Chaiken, S. (1975). "An attributional analysis of the effect of communicator characteristics on opinion change: The case of communicator attractiveness." *Journal of Personality and Social Psychology, 32*, 136-144.

9. Craig, C.S., & McCann, J.M. (1978). "Assessing communication effects on energy conservation." *Journal of Consumer Research, 5*, 82-88.

10. Davis, J. J. (1995). "The effects of message framing on response to environmental communications." *Journalism and Mass Communication Quarterly, 72*, 285-299.

11. Lazarus, R., & Folkman, S. (1984). *Stress, appraisal, and coping.* New York: Springer.

12. McKenzie-Mohr, D., & Dyal, J. (1991). "Perceptions of threat, tactical efficacy and competing threats as determinants of pro-disarmament behavior." *Journal of Social Behavior and Personality, 6*, 675-696.

13. Heckler, S. E. (1994). "The role of memory in understanding and encouraging recycling behavior. Special Issue: Psychology, marketing, and recycling." *Psychology and Marketing, 11*, 375-392.

14. Oskamp, S., Zelezny, L., Schultz, P. W., Hurin, S., Burkhardt, R. & O'Neil, E. (1994). *Commingled versus separated curbside recycling and long-term participation.* Paper presented at the annual conference of the American Psychological Association.

15. Jacobs, H. E., Bailey, J. S., & Crews, J. I. (1984). "Development and analysis of a community-based resource recovery program." *Journal of Applied Behavior Analysis, 17*, 127-145.

16. Folz, D. H. (1991). "Recycling program design, management, and participation: A national survey of municipal experience." *Public Administration Review, 51*, 222-231.

17. Aronson, E., & Gonzales, M.H. (1990). "Alternative social influence processes applied to energy conservation." In J. Edwards, R. S. Tindale, L. Heath, & E. J. Posaval (Eds.), *Social Influences, Processes and Prevention (pp. 301-325)*. New York: Plenum.

18. Bandura, A. (1977). *Social Learning Theory*. Englewood Cliffs, NJ: Prentice-Hall.

19. Winett, R.A., Hatcher, J.W., Fort, T.R., Leckliter, I.N., Love, S.Q., Riley, A.W., & Fishback, J.F. (1982). "The effects of videotape modeling and daily feedback on residential electricity conservation, home temperature and humidity, perceived comfort, and clothing worn: Winter and summer." *Journal of Applied Behavior Analysis, 15,* 381-402.

20. Winett, R.A., Leckliter, I.N., Chinn, D.E., Stahl, B., & Love, S.Q. (1985). "Effects of television modeling on residential energy conservation." *Journal of Applied Behavior Analysis, 18,* 33-44.

21. Burn, S.M. (1991). "Social psychology and the stimulation of recycling behaviors: The block leader approach." *Journal of Applied Social Psychology, 21,* 611-629.

22. Larson, M.E., Houlihan, D., & Goernert, P.N. (1995). "Brief report: Effects of informational feedback on aluminum can recycling." *Behavioral Interventions, 10,* 111-117.

23. Artz, N. & Cooke, P. (2007). "Using E-Mail Listservs to Promote Environmentally Sustainable Behaviors," *Journal of Marketing Communications, 13(4),* 257-276.

24. Seligman, C., & Darley, J. M. (1977). "Feedback as a means of decreasing residential energy consumption." *Journal of Applied Psychology, 62,* 363-368.

25. DeLeon, I. G., & Fuqua, R. W. (1995). "The effects of public commitment and group feedback on curbside recycling." Special Issue: Litter control and recycling. *Environment and Behavior, 27,* 233-250.

26. Rothstein, R. N. (1980). "Television feedback used to modify gasoline consumption." *Behavior Therapy, 11,* 683-688.

INCENTIVES

1. Federation of Canadian Municipalities. *A municipal guide on economic instruments to support municipal waste management programs.* Toronto, Ontario: Resource Integration Systems Ltd. (RIS).

2. Recycling Council of Ontario (1996). *Implementing Garbage User Fees in Ontario.* Toronto, ON: Author.

3. Federation of Canadian Municipalities. *A municipal guide on economic instruments to support municipal waste management programs.* Toronto, ON: Resource Integration Systems Ltd. (RIS).

4. Institute of Applied Research (1980). *Michigan Litter: After.* Sacramento, California: Author.

5. Levitt, L., & Leventhal, G. (1986). "Litter reduction: How effective is the New York State Bottle Bill?" *Environment and Behavior, 18,* 467-479.

6. Centre & South Hastings Recycling Board (1995). *Blue Box 2000: Breaking 50.* Trenton, Ontario.

7. Bamberg, S. (2006). "Is residential relocation a good opportunity to change people's travel behavior? Results From a Theory-Driven Intervention Study." *Environment and Behavior, 38(6),* 820-840.

8. Conn, W.D. (2009). "Applying environmental policy instruments to used oil." *Journal of Environmental Planning and Management, 52(4),* 457–475.

9. Cordeiro, J.J. & Sarkis, J. (2008). "Does explicit contracting effectively link CEO compensation to environmental performance?" *Business Strategy and the Environment, 17,* 304-317.

10. Adachi, C. & Rowlands, I.H. (2010). "The role of policies in supporting the diffusion of solar photovoltaic systems: Experiences from Ontario, Canada's Renewable Energy Standard Offer program." *Sustainability, 2,* 30-47.

11. Abrahamse, W., Steg, L. Vlek, C. & Rothengatter, T. (2005). "A review of intervention studies aimed at household conservation." *Journal of Environmental Psychology, 25,* 273-291.

12. Straka, T.J. Kilgore, M.A., Jacobson, M.G., Greene, J.L. & Daniels, S.E. (2007). "Influence of financial incentives programs in sustaining wildlife values." *Human Dimensions of Wildlife, 12,* 197-199.

13. Sorice, M.G. & Conner, J. R. (2010). "Predicting private landowner intentions to enroll in an incentive program to protect endangered species." *Human Dimensions of Wildlife, 15,* 77-89.

14. Van Vugt, M. (2001). "Community identification moderating the impact of financial incentives in a natural social dilemma: Water conservation." *Personality and Social Psychology Bulletin, 27(11),* 1440-1449.

15. Pucher, J. & Buehler, R. (2008). "Making cycling irresistible: Lessons from the Netherlands, Denmark and Germany." *Transport Reviews, 28(4).* 495-528.

16. Gardner, G. T. & Stern, P.C. (1996). "*Environmental Problems and Human Behavior.*" Boston: Allyn and Bacon.

17. Source unknown

CONVENIENCE

1. McKenzie-Mohr, D., Nemiroff, L. S., Beers, L., & Desmarais, S. (1995). "Determinants of responsible environmental behavior." *Journal of Social Issues, 51,* 139-156.

2. Zuckermann, W. (1992). *End of the Road: From world car crisis to sustainable transportation.* Post Mills, Vermont: Chelsea Green.

3. Hart, S. I. & Spivak, A. L. (1993). *Automobile Dependence and Denial: The elephant in the bedroom.* Pasadena, California: New Paradigm.

4. Crosby, L.A., & Taylor, J.R. (1982). "Consumer satisfaction with Michigan's container deposit - an ecological perspective." *Journal of Marketing, Winter,* 47-60.

5. Shaheen, S., Guzman, S. & Zhang, H. (2010). *Bikesharing in Europe, the Americas, and Asia: Past, present, and future.* Report available online: http://76.12.4.249/artman2/uploads/1/TRB10-Bikesharing.Final.pdf

6. Erlanger, S. (2008). "A fashion catches on in Paris: Cheap bicycle rentals." The New York *Times.* July 13.

7. DeMaio, P. (2009). "Bike-Sharing: History, Impacts, Models of Provision, and Future." *Journal of Public Transportation, 12*, 4, 41-56.

8. Gardner, G. (2010). *Power to the pedals.* World Watch report. Available online at: www.worldwatch.org.

9. Shaheen, S., Guzman, S. & Zhang, H. (2010). *Bikesharing in Europe, the Americas, and Asia: Past, present, and future.* Report available online: http://76.12.4.249/artman2/uploads/1/TRB10-Bikesharing.Final.pdf

10. Waterloo Residential Waste Reduction Unit (1992). *Backyard composter/digester participation pilot study.* Waterloo, Ontario.

PILOTING

1. Lee, N. (2010). "Where's the beef? Social marketing in tough times." *Journal of Social Marketing, 1(1).*

CONCLUDING THOUGHTS

1. Olson, R. (1995). "Sustainability as a social vision." *Journal of Social Issues, 51(4),* 15-35.

About the Author

Dr. Doug McKenzie-Mohr, an environmental psychologist, is the founder of community-based social marketing, and his best-selling book, *Fostering Sustainable Behavior: An Introduction to Community-Based Social Marketing*, has become requisite reading for those who deliver programs to promote sustainable behavior. He has worked internationally with a diverse array of governmental and non-governmental agencies, assisting them in identifying the barriers to behavior change and in developing and evaluating community-based social marketing initiatives to overcome these barriers. He has served as an advisor for Canada's public education efforts on climate change, as the coordinator of the international organization, Holis: The Society for a Sustainable Future, and as a member of Canada's National Round Table on the Environment and the Economy. He is a former Professor of Psychology at St. Thomas University in New Brunswick, Canada where he co-coordinated the Environment and Society program. More than 50,000 program managers have attended workshops on community-based social marketing that he has delivered internationally.

If you have enjoyed *Fostering Sustainable Behavior*, you might also enjoy other

BOOKS TO BUILD A NEW SOCIETY

Our books provide positive solutions for people who want
to make a difference. We specialize in:

Sustainable Living • Green Building • Peak Oil • Renewable Energy
Environment & Economy • Natural Building & Appropriate Technology
Progressive Leadership • Resistance and Community
Educational and Parenting Resources

New Society Publishers

ENVIRONMENTAL BENEFITS STATEMENT

New Society Publishers has chosen to produce this book on recycled
paper made with 100% post consumer waste, processed chlorine free,
and old growth free.

For every 5,000 books printed, New Society Publishers saves the
following resources:[1]

25	Trees
2,291	Pounds of Solid Waste
2,521	Gallons of Water
3,288	Kilowatt Hours of Electricity
4,164	Pounds of Greenhouse Gases
18	Pounds of HAPs, VOCs, and AOX Combined
6	Cubic Yards of Landfill Space

---

[1]Environmental benefits are calculated based on research done by the Environmental
Defense Fund and the other members of the Paper Task Force who studied the
environmental impacts of the paper industry.

For a full list of NSP's titles, please call 1-800-567-6772
or check out our website at: www.newsociety.com

NEW SOCIETY PUBLISHERS
www.newsociety.com